Henry Wood

Natural law in the business world

Henry Wood

Natural law in the business world

ISBN/EAN: 9783337712204

Printed in Europe, USA, Canada, Australia, Japan

Cover: Foto ©Suzi / pixelio.de

More available books at **www.hansebooks.com**

NATURAL LAW

IN THE

BUSINESS WORLD.

BY

HENRY WOOD.

"Of Law, there can be no less acknowledged than that her seat is the bosom of God, her voice the harmony of the world: all things in heaven and earth do her homage, the very least as feeling her care, and the greatest as not exempted from her power."

RICHARD HOOKER, 1553–1600.

BOSTON:
LEE AND SHEPARD, PUBLISHERS.
NEW YORK:
CHARLES T. DILLINGHAM.
1887.

PREFACE.

IN presenting this little volume to the public, the writer makes no claim to any new discoveries, or original theories in the domain of Political Economy; nor has he any ambition to enter into philosophical or theoretical speculations. An honest effort to trace out the working and application of Natural Law, as it runs through the economic and social fabric, in a plain and simple, though it is hoped practical manner, is all that is attempted.

Economic works by theorists and specialists have been multiplied to such an extent, that it seems almost presumptuous for one who has had only a practical business training to venture into a field already so thoroughly explored. It is, however, the belief of the writer, that in a great majority of recent works, the sure, continuous, and unerring operation of certain fixed principles, and their resultant effects, has been greatly overlooked or ignored, and sentimental and impractical theories have been substituted for them.

Such a variety of new plans, radical changes, and "reforms" have been proposed, in order to improve existing conditions, that the world must be re-made in order to give them an opportunity to be tried.

Fixed and immutable laws must be bent or broken so as to fit and harmonize with pet theories and individual prejudices. Is it not the better way to make some effort to detect and bring to light the lines along which these natural and fundamental principles are operative, and then look for improvement by striving to put ourselves more nearly in harmony with them? If they are irreversible and continuous, let us make peace with them, rather than provoke a conflict. The ills of our social system, the hardships of labor, and the inequalities of fortune cannot be got rid of by any short-cut route of social revolution, or industrial transformation. Circumstances and conditions may change, but principles never. Wealth has always been the natural sequence to industry, temperance, and perseverance, and it will always so continue.

In regard to the labor question, the writer will yield to no one in respect to his sympathy for, and interest in the laboring man, but he looks for his improvement and elevation in an entirely different direction from the majority of those who claim to especially champion his cause. There can be no active antagonism between different wheels of the same machine, without disastrous results to all. The true ideal of society is a complete and rounded unity, but this unity is made up of variety. Like the different parts of a vast mechanism, this variety must be harmonious.

The plain words of this book are in no sense directed against labor, but only against the abuses and evils that masquerade under its banner. Class prejudice, so persistently stimulated by some agitators, is disastrous to business confidence and prosperity. Demand for labor and products cannot be coerced, but harmony will stimulate and increase it. Our object in this work is to promote the interest of labor, which is the interest of society. We endeavor to point out the natural and solid highway to success, through industry, merit, and economy, and how to avoid the treacherous quagmires of antagonism, coercion, and tyranny, which end in business stagnation and idleness. The conclusions arrived at are not mere matters of choice, but the logical result of unchanging natural principles. We acknowledge our indebtedness for facts and statistics to the writings of Adam Smith, J. S. Mill, Ricardo, the Duke of Argyll, W. Stanley Jevons, John B. Jervis, Prof. A. T. Hadley, Prof. F. A. Walker, Edward Atkinson, W. B. Weeden, and C. S. Ashley.

The substance of a few of the following chapters has appeared in occasional articles in the public press.

CONTENTS.

		PAGE
I.	General Principles	11
II.	Supply and Demand	21
III.	Labor, Laborers, and Production	35
IV.	Labor Combinations and their Effect on the Laborer	51
V.	Socialism	77
VI.	Dependence and Poverty	89
VII.	Employers and their Duties	97
VIII.	State Arbitration	109
IX.	Can Capital and Labor be harmonized?	117
X.	Economic Legislation and its Proper Limits	129
XI.	Wealth, and its Unequal Distribution	145
XII.	Centralization of Business	161
XIII.	Alternations of Prosperity and Depression	173
XIV.	Railroads, and Railroad Consolidation	187
XV.	The Corporation	205
XVI.	Conclusion	215

GENERAL PRINCIPLES.

"*Mark what unvaried laws preserve each state,
Laws wise as nature, and as fixed as fate.*"
Pope.

"*There is a higher law than the constitution.*"
William H. Seward.

"*All are but parts of one stupendous whole,
Whose body nature is, and God the soul.*"
Pope.

I.

GENERAL PRINCIPLES.

IN order to make any real progress in the study of Natural Law, it is imperative that we should divest ourselves of all prejudices, pet theories, and predilections, and preserve a frame of mind that is thoroughly impartial. We must make an unbiassed and persistent search for existing orders of events, and consecutive occurrences, as they already are, rather than as we would like to find them. If the facts do not conform to our preconceived ideas, we must beware of trying to bend or break them in order to produce a seeming harmony or conformity. For example, several recent writers have made an effort to suspend or abolish the natural law of competition, especially as applied to labor. This principle does not fit into their ideal system, and must therefore be set aside. It is bad policy to pick a quarrel with established truths, and in such a conflict, one is likely to emerge from it in much the same condition as Don Quixote found himself after his combat with the wind-mill. In order to arrive at right conclusions, a candid and patient search for truth is necessary, even if it upsets our cherished plans and desires. The principle of competition as applied to labor may seem cruel and offensive, but if it is a natural one, let us recognize it, and try to discover whether there are not other laws in operation which will have the effect to modify or counteract its apparently undesirable features, and so let it keep its place, where it has some good use as an essential factor in a complete system.

Natural Law, as applied to the domain of Political Economy, is defined by Webster as "a rule of conduct arising out of the natural relations of human beings, established by the Creator, and existing prior to any positive precept." Natural Law in the business world is not a different law from that which runs through physics or morals, mechanics or chemistry. It is but one of the many subdivisions of Universal Natural Law, or the grand Unity of Truth. In other words, the principles which reign in the department of economics are not artificially fenced off in a field by themselves, but they have a most intimate connection with all the other subdivisions of orderly facts. There is also a corresponding kinship in error. With false premises and a colored medium, not only one truth is transformed, but all its relations are also distorted and colored, so that all are apparently of the same general hue. In this way systems of error are built up, for with one error for a starting point, a whole series must be evolved to harmonize with it.

The lines of Natural Law in the business world may not be so clear cut and mathematical in their character as are those in some other parts of the general field, but the evidence of their existence is just as perfect and convincing. They are so interlaced and mingled with human or legislative law on the one hand, and with a purely mental and moral economy on the other, that any study of one is impossible, except in connection with the others. They shade into each other so perfectly that no line of demarcation is visible. The general perception of the uniform and universal reign of law has grown with the growth of knowledge, and at the present time the highest aim of science is its fuller discovery, classification, and interpretation. Natural Law is but another name for the expressions and methods of the Creator. That being the case, it is evident that all just and wholesome human enactments must be founded upon it. That this true foundation is more generally recognized and built upon at the present time than in any past age, is obvious; and this is especially the case where constitutional and democratic forms of government prevail. Human law and legislation is the will of society, and although it may put limits on individual will, it is yet indispensable to human welfare. The communistic dream of a possible ideal condition of society can never be realized, for the reason that man is naturally selfish. Such conditions could only be successful on a planet where unselfishness is the normal condition. There has been a steady improvement in human laws and government, in just the proportion that Natural Law has been understood and interpreted. Step by step the patriarchal, tribal, and various other forms of government have played their part, and have led up to the modern state, which is the most wholesome condition of society yet evolved. Further improvement will follow in proportion as the lines of Natural Law shall be wrought into the warp and woof of the social fabric. The key to progress, completeness, and approximate perfection in every department, whether physical, mental, moral, or even spiritual (as Prof. Drummond has so ably demonstrated in his book "Natural Law in the Spiritual World"), is conformity to law. Take a few illustrations: A thorough observance of hygienic law tends directly to healthful, normal, and perfect bodily development. A greater or less transgression brings a proportionate penalty. The penalty must be paid whether the violation be knowingly or ignorantly committed. A headache and nervous depression are very certain to follow a prolonged drunken revelry, but no more so than are panic and business stagnation to come after an era of wild speculation. That physical disease, the effect of which is to gradually thin the blood toward a watery basis, when it continues unchecked, is no less certain in its logical results than will be the degradation of our monetary system to a silver basis, if the process of dilution indefinitely continues. Erroneous legislation may for a while prevent the full assertion of this law, but it is nevertheless an active, living force, and is unceasingly pressing in the direction of its natural and logical fulfilment. A stream may be dammed on its way to the ocean, but the final tide-level of its waters is not a matter of question. It would be as reasonable to expect to increase the efficiency of one blade of a pair of shears by the mutilation of its companion, as to try to benefit either capital or labor by an antagonistic policy toward the other. Illustrations might be multiplied.

Men often feel that they can transgress natural principles with impunity so long as they avoid the open violation and penalty of human legislation, forgetting that the penalty of the former is even more certain, and is the inevitable sequence of the transgression. They may try to persuade themselves that even eternal principles are elastic and subject to exceptions, for the reason that they sometimes seem to fail to at once assert themselves. One thing, however, is certain. If they apparently fail to vindicate themselves speedily, we may be sure that they are always pressing in that direction, and will never be satisfied till the end is reached. We confine water in a tube, but its tendency to seek a level continues, and no human power can divest it of this inclination. Natural Law is a living force, persistent, reliable, and always in its place and pressing to do its work. It is this very certainty and invariableness that enables us to use it, and to make it serve us. While, therefore, it is true that we are always under its sovereignty, it is no less true that when we make its acquaintance, and comply with its conditions, it becomes our most valuable and indispensable servant. Its powerful aid, like that of steam or electricity, is always at our service, only we must not dictate its methods of operation. We make mistakes, and our lines of action cross each other, while its operations are harmonious. They may counteract or modify each other, but never oppose, for truth cannot be in opposition to truth. The only warfare it wages is with error, and the conflict is an unceasing one.

SUPPLY AND DEMAND.

> *"All are needed by each one;
> Nothing is fair or good alone."*
>
> *Emerson.*

II.

SUPPLY AND DEMAND.

THE law of supply and demand is perhaps the most general and fundamental of all the brotherhood of natural laws, and we have direct relations with it at all times and under all circumstances. It lies at the foundation of all modern commerce, civilization, invention, and science. It has been the main-spring and impelling force in every transaction, trade, or exchange, back to the time when man existed under the most primitive conditions. It was the basis of the first exchanges of flint arrowheads and skins of wild beasts among savage and barbarous tribes, as it is also of all the endless and multiform currents and countercurrents of modern economic life and society. Its force cannot be measured. Its pressure impels mankind to work its behests, in gathering, transporting, and exchanging the products of the globe, in order that these two principles may meet and satisfy each other. Men will penetrate to the heart of tropical Africa, or to the iceberg regions of the Arctic zone, they will dive to the bottom of the sea, or delve in the bowels of the earth, to bring forth all the complex materials of supply, in order to make them equal to the grand aggregate of universal demand. No enterprise is too venturesome, no effort too daring. These two elements are like two halves of a sphere, neither complete without the other, and each waiting for and needing the other, as necessary to produce roundness and perfection. In the economy of the creation each of these factors is not only incomplete without the other, but each is evidence of the existence of the other. Even in the spiritual world, which is more beyond our comprehension, universal analogy teaches that as man was created with a natural desire or demand for future existence, that demand will be supplied. In general, demand was created for supply, and supply for demand, and they have a strong and unerring affinity for each other. A vacuum is a demand for air, and cold for heat. Man's natural constitution has many demands, and these are supplied when it is in a normal condition.

Applying these principles more specifically, let us take the problem of meeting the food demands of a great city like London or New York. Supplies of just the required amount and variety are forthcoming from every quarter of the globe, and all without any system, design, or forethought. The Chinaman is gathering the tea, the Brazilian the coffee, the Dakota farmer is raising the wheat; and every other quarter and country of the globe is working and striving to make up the supply to fit this demand. It does fit it as perfectly as if it were regulated by a pair of colossal balances. The element of price comes in and smooths off all the inequalities, so that the two surfaces come together as perfectly as though polished for the purpose. If a temporary, or even expected surplus of any article occurs, the price drops just enough to increase the demand to the point of perfect equilibrium. If there is a temporary or foreseen future deficiency, the price rises, and the inevitable equilibrium is restored as before. It is the element of price that always determines the point at which that is reached, and price is modified by still another element, which is competition. In the event of a tendency toward excess, competition takes place among sellers; and, on the other hand, a predominance of demand causes competition among buyers. All commercial transactions and prices, not only of material products, but of everything that bears price, like rates of interest, rents, salaries, brain work, as well as muscle work, are so regulated. The salary of the clergyman, the fees of the lawyer, and rates of transportation, as well as the rate of wages for manual labor, are all controlled by this law. A high order of talent brings a high price from its scarcity. Price is a relative and not an abstract quantity. Competition among buyers may cause strawberries to bring a dollar a quart in April, and among sellers may bring them down to ten cents in June. They were relatively as cheap at the one time as at the other, the price at which supply and demand became equal varying by so much in the different months.

These laws are elastic and beneficent, and they adapt themselves to all conditions in a natural and easy way, if allowed to run smoothly and without interference. Not that they will do away with all the ills of society, or give to every man employment at good wages, or always give success in business, for all these drawbacks are incidental to human fallibility and imperfection. The effect, however, of any attempt to put any forced or artificial laws in their place is to increase the friction and difficulties tenfold. It always reacts, and is harmful to those who mistakenly hoped for benefit.

A few illustrations: Legislative interference in trying to fix rates of interest (or, rather, one might say, to take away the freedom of individual contract), in the different States, is now generally admitted to be worse than useless, although years ago it was regarded as necessary. The effort to substitute artificial rates for natural ones, under penalty, not only did not accomplish the purpose intended, but actually made interest dearer, by obstructing supplies, injuring confidence, and by natural reaction. When the peculiar conditions in any State made money really worth more than the maximum legal rate, the practical rate would be still further enhanced, to equal the risk of penalty incurred by the lender. Both parties would also feel that they did no moral wrong by evading a statute which interfered with the first principles of personal freedom. So generally has this view of the case come to prevail, that this form of legislative interference with Natural Law is practically a dead letter, though in some States the ill-advised statutes are still nominally in force. Legislative interference with rates of transportation, and with passenger, telegraph, and telephone service, is in the same line, and in the long run will be found to produce similar results. Aside from legislative interference (which will be more fully considered in the chapter on Economic Legislation), the most formidable attempts to force artificial prices occur in the cases of railway pools or combinations, speculative corners in food products and coal, and in labor unions. The results of these efforts are in the main unsuccessful, and in any case but temporary, and they, of course, lack the moral dignity of legislative interference. In the case of railway combinations, statistics show that in all instances where pool rates were put at a point much above that which may be regarded as the normal, they have been very short-lived. Such a variety of disintegrating and competitive influences come in, that even the most binding agreements to maintain artificial rates soon have to yield. In the case of speculative combinations and corners, or efforts to control market prices, it may be admitted that in a few cases they have been apparently successful, but in a vastly greater number they have not succeeded, and often they have ruined their projectors. In the successful cases, where one clique of operators have succeeded in cornering the market, or in establishing artificial prices, it has been in consequence of another clique selling or agreeing to sell what they did not possess (in common parlance of the commercial world called short selling), which is in itself an abnormal condition. Any effort to artificially advance prices against natural consumption alone is rarely attempted, for to have any chance for success there must be the opposing clique of "short sellers," or those who are trying to artificially depress the market. Even with the large amount of "short selling," attempts to corner the market are becoming more and more infrequent, owing to the increased rapidity of transportation and communication, which has a strong equalizing tendency. Wherever such combinations have temporarily succeeded, the result has been brought about by peculiar conditions, and in a forcible manner, before Natural Law had time to assert itself. It was like lifting a heavy weight in spite of gravitation.

There is much popular misapprehension on this subject. We often see newspaper headlines like the following: "The West is holding back its grain," or "Chicago speculators are trying to force up the foreign markets," or "Wall Street has combined to get up a boom," and many other similar announcements, instances of which might be multiplied. The idea that the millions of farmers in the West, or that the thousands of operators in Chicago or Wall Street, could come to any general understanding in regard to a uniform policy is absurd. Instead of any such condition of unity ever existing, there are always two parties, known in common parlance as "bulls" and "bears," each of which is a balance to the other, like the two elements under consideration. The bears represent the principle of supply, and the bulls that of demand; and, as elsewhere, the higher or lower prices determine the point of equilibrium between them. So far from combination, not only each party, but every *individual* in each party, is trying to excel all others in making the most correct estimate of the natural drift and tendency of existing conditions, and how to profit thereby.

Of attempted forced artificial prices for labor by labor unions, we shall speak more fully in another chapter, but in passing will suggest that the uniform dominion of these principles does not abruptly terminate here, as some of the sentimental theorists maintain. They are obliged to assume that it does make an exception in this spot, in order to save their system. No matter how much we might wish it otherwise, facts are opposed. Not only that, but upon closer study we shall find that the laboring man is as much concerned in the integrity of these laws, even if he had the power to modify them, as any other part of society. As we have before noticed, the prices of brain labor are regulated by these two elements, and it would be a violation of all analogy to claim any exception in the case of muscle. He who tries to sow the seeds of discontent in the minds of laboring men by teaching such a theory, is not their true friend. He may be actuated by an honest, though misguided sympathy, but it is none the less harmful to the laborer, and tends directly to degrade his manliness and independence. Those sentimentalists who expect the laboring man will be benefited by force of combination (as though he were going into a combat) are on the wrong track. Societies of laboring men might be organized for social, intellectual, and moral purposes, and be productive of great good; but when, as at present, they are constituted for the sole purpose of forcing artificial prices, they injure not only the laborer himself, but they are harmful to business and confidence, and an injury to society at large. A seller of labor, or any other commodity, is dependent on demand, and demand cannot be coerced. Whenever that is attempted, it shrinks back. It is like picking a quarrel with the only friend that can help us. It would be a poor way to induce a horse to drink, to force his head under water.

Demand can be stimulated, courted, and increased by the adoption of such a policy as will promote peaceful conditions, and inspire confidence, present and future. Wages will then rise *naturally* from increased demand. Under such conditions, every employer would want to enlarge his capacity, and as a buyer of labor would have to offer higher prices to get it. The almost or quite one hundred per cent advance in average wages which has been made during the last thirty years, in spite of the immense immigration into the country, is a natural advance, and was caused by an excess of demand. If the forcing process had been continually applied during that period, the advance would have been much less marked, for the reason that the demand would have been injured. As we have already seen that supply and demand are always equal, it follows that an injury to the one is harmful to both. It may be objected that in the case of factory towns and cities, the immobility of labor would prevent in some degree the right adjustment of wages by the law of supply and demand. This sounds rather plausible, but, in the first place, there is no other adjustment possible; therefore, we have no choice. In the next place, the practical immobility is never so great, but that in the event of any forced or continued attempt to impose artificially low prices upon labor by employers, a gradual but sure process of recovery would at once begin, and would not rest until the normal rate was approximated. The emigration from such a factory or town might be slow, but it would be continuous, until the inevitable equilibrium was reached. It would be no compliment to the intelligence and manliness of laboring men to assert to the contrary. The real self-interest of the employer would also become a factor, for the emigration would be from his most intelligent and desirable class of help.

In general, demand has grown from the few and simple cravings of primitive man for mere food and shelter, and these of the simplest character, up to the infinite and wonderfully complex variety of desire that characterizes modern civilization, and supply has paralleled its track for the entire distance. This equal progress and enlargement of supply and demand will continue in the future, and no one can fix its limits.

LABOR, LABORERS, AND PRODUCTION.

"*He that by the plough would thrive
Himself must either hold or drive.*"

"*Man goeth forth unto his work and to his labor until the evening.*"

Ps. civ. 23.

"*On bravely through the sunshine and the showers,
Time hath his work to do and we have ours.*"

Emerson.

III.

LABOR, LABORERS, AND PRODUCTION.

LABOR is normal; idleness, abnormal. The physical, mental, and moral faculties of man were created for use and exercise, and it is only by their active training that they attain skill, efficiency, and excellence. That the active employment of the gifts and capabilities of man's nature was designed by the Creator is abundantly proved, both by analogy and experience. As all human happiness and perfection are reached in the line of conformity to law, so a non-conformity brings misery and unhappiness. Labor is a blessing, and idleness a curse. Human powers must have occupation, or else they become weakened, withered, and out of harmony. As mankind is at present constituted, it were better to give him the barren and sterile soil bringing forth weeds and thistles, to be transformed by the healthful activity of his energy into blooming gardens and fruitful fields, than to supply him with all these delightful and useful objects spontaneously, and without effort and toil on his part.

The world is full of things to be done, and labor is, therefore, the most staple of all commodities. The mistake of thinking that the hands alone perform labor is a very common one, when the fact is, that every part and power of the body and mind can and does labor and toil, and only by this activity can it fulfil its function. Under primitive conditions, there was a general activity of body and mind, rather than a special development in any one direction. The barbarian was his own tailor, carpenter, jeweller, farmer, and common carrier, and his products were few and poor. Under modern conditions, activity is more subdivided, and education more thorough. Thus, we have farmers, carpenters, painters, engravers, masons, and numberless other trades and professions, each one of whom has special education, and as a result, superiority. Each therefore does not only his own particular kind of work for himself, but for all the others, because his production is far more perfect. So in the department of brain labor, the clergyman, physician, lawyer, banker, scientist, historian, and statesman have all cultivated their powers in their several fields to a high state of efficiency, and each has his place in the rounding out and completing of the grand unit called society. In this consists the great superiority of the modern state, with its high degree of civilization, over the barbarous governments and peoples of primitive times and conditions.

The scientist, historian, and bookkeeper are as truly laborers and producers as he who handles a pick, plough, or loom. The popular use of the term "labor" as applied only to those who exercise muscle, is therefore erroneous. The brakeman in the employment of a railway company may, by industry, energy, and ability, rise to be its president, but he is no less a laborer than before, and as a man, not necessarily any more worthy or noble.

While a normal amount of labor is in accord with law, and is necessary to healthful and harmonious development, an excess of exertion is harmful. It is also obvious to any close observer that, of the two, an excess of mental labor is more wearing and disastrous in its results on the health and constitution than is too much physical exertion. The care, worry, and responsibility incidental to mental occupations cause vast numbers to break down in health; and here again the popular idea is at fault that connects all hardship and suffering with only manual occupations. While therefore our sympathy may go out towards the laborer who uses a shovel for eight or ten hours in a day, we should not entirely overlook the weary bookkeeper or clerk, who often works twelve or fourteen hours, amidst unwholesome conditions and impure air. The sleep of the man who labors with muscle is sweeter, his digestion more sure, and his vigor greater than that of the average brain laborer. The idea that manual labor is in itself degrading, and to be avoided as far as is possible, is the delusion of the present time.

The ideal man would be he whose physical, mental, and moral powers are all well rounded out, cultivated, and harmoniously balanced. Idleness is a violation of Natural Law, and its companions in transgression are improvidence, degradation, intemperance, and decay. By inexorable law and logic, each positive virtue has its corresponding opposite condition of vice and error.

As to the different varieties of labor, it may be said that all are indispensable, the mental as well as the physical, each in its proper sphere. The steam in the locomotive is a more subtle and refined factor than the boiler and wheels, but no less necessary and important. So the brain worker, though in a more delicate, refined, and nominally higher sphere, is only a component part of a general system, but in personality is not necessarily above his fellow-laborer. The test of excellency of a wheel in a machine is that it fills well its peculiar place and office. There is no natural aristocracy of the mental laborer over the physical that is based upon his greater necessity to society, for Natural Law is not sentimental, but thoroughly democratic.

Having found that labor is natural, necessary, and in harmony with man's constitution, let us consider its object. In the economy of Natural Law, means are always in order to an end. Labor is the means; production, the result or object. The finished building is as much the product of the architect as of the carpenter or mason; or, rather, it is the joint product of both. In the distinction made between mental and manual labor, it is evident that only the predominant element is referred to, for neither can be strictly pure. The simplest manual task must be accompanied by a mental process: and likewise, the scholar or scientist must do some physical labor with pen or apparatus.

Production is only a general term for food, clothing, home, education, surplus. These constitute wealth, which is only another name for accumulated labor. The wages paid for labor are rather the above-named objects, than any certain sum of money, for the value of money consists only in the products that it will command. The natural aim and object then of the laborer is to increase the result produced by his labor. How can this be done? First, personally, or by a greater activity and industry, and by the cultivation of individual qualities which tend to success. Second, by surrounding himself with more favorable environment and conditions. It is not only in accord with Natural Law, but with common-sense, that individual energy and ambition and persistent training in a particular department are necessary for much progress in any line of effort. The question with the wage-worker must not be, how few hours or how little exertion can I possibly get along with? but rather, how much can I accomplish? He who puts forth his best efforts will soon become indispensable to his employer, and his labor will naturally rise in value, and he will soon by positive development step into the ranks of the employer himself.

Society is composed of two classes, the independent and the dependent. The question as to which of these two classes a man will belong is, under all ordinary conditions, a matter of individual choice. The road to independence is open, and finger-boards are up on every corner. Here is seen one of the bad effects on the laborer of labor unions. Instead of relying upon individual merit and energy for maintaining or advancing his wages, he relies upon the power of the union. The former is natural; the latter, artificial. By this course he loses his motive for the attainment of personal superiority and natural advancement, and settles down to the dead level of the dependent elements that surround and control him.

The goal of the American laborer is the position of accumulated labor, or, in other words, that of capitalist. A continuous, even if a small margin between income and expenditure in one direction fixes the condition of independence, and, in the other, of its necessary opposite. It is not a matter of chance, but of law. In this country, even if a laborer begins in the dependent ranks, his condition is not a fixed one. The transition to the independent class is easy and plain, when the natural course of individual merit and effort is chosen. Examples on every hand prove that this is universal experience, and is not a matter of sentiment or theory. But a very small part of the wealth of this country was inherited, probably nine tenths being the result of personal labor. Any short-cut route to success is very uncertain, and any forced march, outside of the natural conditions of progress, or under a dictator, is generally disastrous. But the broad, direct, and solid highway of individual industry, economy, and temperance is always open. A surplus is what the daily wage-worker should be accumulating, and presently it supplements his personal force with power of another kind. For such a man to try to antagonize accumulated labor, or those who possess it, is to oppose the very principles and conditions which are his own hope and reward.

The young American wage-worker who puts forth his best efforts, and who practises what economists call abstinence, or the limiting of expenditure to less than income, has as good ground for expecting to become a capitalist as has the gardener to expect a crop from good seed deposited in a rich and fertile soil. It is no less true that he who does as little as will possibly keep him in his position, and who has little regard for the interests of his employer, has the elements in him that make it almost certain that he will always be a member of the dependent class.

In regard to means favorable to increased production by labor which are external to the laborer, two general conditions may be mentioned: first, by increasing the efficiency of mechanical appliances and aids; and second, by seeking a favorable location or propitious field for operations. As to the first, it is not long since that labor-saving machines were looked upon as the enemy of the laboring man, and some of the most useful inventions were forcibly destroyed, and their owners persecuted. Even as recently as thirty or forty years ago, the opinion was quite prevalent in the rural districts of New England that the general advent of railroads would quite destroy the value of both horses and oats. It was found later that the world needed them both, and the result was just the opposite of what the farmers had expected.

When the printing press was first brought into use, it was found that with it one man could do the work of two hundred copyists, and, as a consequence, it was feared that one hundred and ninety-nine men would be thrown out of employment. But notice the result. Soon the superiority of printed books over those that were written, together with the lower price, stimulated authorship and increased the sale and use of books a thousand-fold, and employment was given to more printers than there were copyists before. Besides this direct result, there were in addition the related occupations of paper makers, bookbinders, book sellers, and various others, so that the final result was the employment of many times the number of persons that seemingly lost their occupation at the time the invention came into practical use. And this, as a result, merely of an economic process, aside from the immense impetus given by it to human learning, art, and knowledge. It may be regarded as in accordance with Natural Law that every new invention and improvement that saves manual labor, and adds to the comfort and convenience of mankind, at the same time increases and opens up new avenues of employment, so that, as in the instance just given, it gives occupation to greater numbers of operatives than were before required. Every such new improvement increases the production, the varieties of occupation, and also raises the grade of employment. The engineer who runs a locomotive is in a higher grade of occupation than he who wields a pick, for the reason that there is more of the intellectual element in it. The higher grade is in the occupation, for the man that uses the pick is not necessarily lower as a man.

In general, therefore, with the progress of science and invention, mind has more and more asserted its supremacy over matter, and the physical exertion of the laborer has been mixed and tempered in an increasing degree with the intellectual. As man becomes better acquainted with Natural Law, he gains in his supremacy and command of the material elements around him, and makes them minister to his complex needs and desires. All this is to the special advantage and benefit of the manual laborer. In consequence of this, the humble cottager of to-day has more of comfort and even luxury than the king in his palace could have enjoyed three hundred years ago. It is said that Queen Elizabeth wore the first pair of knit stockings ever brought to England, and they were regarded as a great luxury, while now even a beggar could hardly be found without them. The introduction and use of the telegraph, telephone, and other electrical appliances afford examples of the conveniences now enjoyed by all classes. These, at the same time, open up immense fields and new avenues for human energy and employment. As before suggested, labor becomes more efficient in production by subdivision. The Jack-at-all-trades style of production belongs to a past age, but the present tendency is towards perfection of detail, by means of thorough organization and subdivision.

The law of progress is in the line of each member of society doing the particular thing that he can do best, and leaving everything else alone. This natural principle is being more widely utilized than ever before, and, as a result, no past age can be compared with the present in respect to ease, quantity, and quality of production.

Our own country, without doubt, presents a field of operation where the greatest possible production can be had for a given amount of labor. The American youth have before them the most promising opportunities that have ever been enjoyed in any age or country. They are indebted for this, not only to the fact that they have command of all the accumulated skill, knowledge, and experience of their predecessors, but that all their natural rights and privileges are secured to them by the beneficent care and protection of our free government. They start in the race without any of the impediments that pertain to less democratic conditions. In the Old World, the fixedness of class, rank, and position, together with systems of entail, compulsory military service, and many other influences which are artificial in their character, are dead-weights, and in opposition to the free exercise of Natural Law.

LABOR COMBINATIONS AND THEIR EFFECT ON THE LABORER.

"*Every tub must stand on its own bottom.*"

"*The truth shall make you free.*"
John viii. 32.

"*They made and recorded a sort of institute and digest of anarchy, called the Rights of Man.*"
Burke.

IV.

LABOR COMBINATIONS AND THEIR EFFECT ON THE LABORER.

IN examining the claims of labor organizations, let it be understood that we take them as they are, and not as they might be. It is freely admitted that societies of working men might be formed for purposes that would be highly beneficial and praiseworthy. Reading and literary organizations, lyceums for debate, societies for the promotion of temperance and morals, scientific and trade associations having for their object the increase of technical knowledge in the various occupations and professions, — all these, and others that might be named, would be of the greatest advantage and benefit to working men. But labor combinations as they exist give little or no attention to these grand possibilities.

Their entire action and effort is in the direction of vainly trying to combat the natural principle of supply and demand.

Let us look at this matter in detail. Why are these combinations an injury to working men?

First. Because their foundation and mainspring is the idea of antagonism to capital, or accumulated labor.

Second. Because their influence is against the exercise of individual merit, industry, and excellence, and distinctly in the direction of dependency.

Third. Personal freedom of action and contract is surrendered to the control of others, whose judgment is often faulty and prejudiced.

Fourth. They are tyrannical in their action toward all unorganized laborers.

Fifth. Their logical tendency and influence is in the general direction of socialism.

Let us examine these points in order as above mentioned.

First. Their foundation and main-spring is the idea of antagonism to capital, or accumulated labor.

The idea of the necessary existence of this sentimental enmity has been most industriously promulgated, and this, combined with a degree of jealousy in human nature toward those whom we imagine to be better off than ourselves, has given popular currency to this feeling. It has become such a habit to speak of the "interest of labor," and of the "interest of capital," assuming that each is opposed to the other, that we adopt the practice without thinking of its utter fallacy and absurdity. The fact is, there is no natural antagonism, because both are mutual allies and necessary helps to each other. When one suffers, both suffer; and when one is prosperous, both are. There is no more sense in a quarrel between them than there would be between the right and left hands, or between two wheels of the same machine. To talk about a conflict between them is a pure invention. As well talk about a quarrel between brick laying and commerce, or industry and banking. Persons may disagree, but occupations, conditions, and truths, never; for they are all parts of one natural and harmonious whole.

There are many leaders, organizers, agitators, and politicians whose interests lie directly in the line of keeping up this harmful and expensive fallacy. The machinery of labor organizations gives them many opportunities to gratify ambition, love of notoriety, sense of power and authority, or to seek financial benefit and political capital. We wish to be perfectly fair and just to gentlemen occupying official positions in the Knights of Labor and kindred organizations, and make no charge that any are influenced by the considerations just named. We are discussing principles, and not men. No doubt many are interested in this work who are conscientious, and who sincerely feel that they are doing the cause of labor a great good. Here comes in a principle before mentioned. With one error for a basis, a whole group of allied errors have to be evolved to harmonize with it in order to form a system. Assuming that capital and labor are enemies, and not allies, the logical result would be combination, offensive and defensive, with close ranks, thorough discipline, and perfect equipment for warfare.

If there were no capitalists, there would be no factories, mills, railroads, machinery, or wages. How can capital be our enemy when its absence from society would throw us back into a state of barbarism? Without it, we could not travel by rail or by sea, or have anything to wear, except what we made with our own hands. Its enterprise enlarges the field of operations, increases the demand for labor, and enhances its market value.

The sentimental theorists who have written on political economy ought to see that their teachings are contrary to the eternal principles of economic science; but the difficulty seems to be that their business education has been entirely theoretical. It would be an interesting experiment if some of these writers on "Labor Problems" would embark in real business. Let one take the management of a large manufacturing corporation, another the control of some railroad system, and a third assume the direction of affairs in a large importing or jobbing house. If consistent, they should conduct these various kinds of business on the sentimental basis. In hiring their help, they should not be governed by the market price of labor, but should pay inefficient men the same as those of the best grade, provided they had as large families, or rather, perhaps, the price fixed by the local "district organization." They should pay ten hours' wages for eight hours' work, and employ none but union men, even if others should starve. The mercantile manager should handle nothing but union goods, even if just as good non-union articles could be had for ten per cent less. The railroad manager should have no locomotives on his road, unless they were made in every part by union hands; and if his switchmen struck, he should not hire any other good men that applied for work at the market price. He should grant the terms asked by the strikers, and take them back, even if he knew that they would strike again the next day. If he wished to change his rules, hours, or methods, he should first get permission from the nearest "member of the executive board," whether that official knew anything of the nature of the business or not; and his negotiations should be entirely with this official, and not with the men themselves. It is very probable that in each of the supposed cases a year's trial of sentimental management would be ample to satisfy the respective stockholders in regard to its merits, as compared with real business methods. It is one thing to assume business conditions, suited to a theoretical treatise, and quite another to act under those conditions in real life. The cases supposed would be only putting in practice the every-day claims and theories of labor organizations. Suppose that the commerce of cities and nations was conducted on this basis as an experiment. We can imagine that it would not long continue before both laborer and employer would cry out for another Adam Smith, to lead us back to the solid ground of natural principles.

The prejudice of the wage-worker has been wrought upon until he has been made to feel that it is necessary for him to go into a strong combination for his own safety and protection. Capital has been personified before him as an unscrupulous, overbearing, and rich opponent, who is doing his utmost to crush and degrade him, and with such a picture before him his antagonism is naturally aroused. Such impressions are mischievous and harmful to the best interests of both parties.

Second. Their influence is against the exercise of individual merit, industry, and excellence, and distinctly in the direction of dependency.

It is almost self-evident, that when a man depends upon the organization of which he is a member to maintain or advance his wages, rather than on his own individual merits, he is on the downward road toward dependency.

Good honest muscle, skill, and energy are the most staple of all commodities, and they will rarely fail to find a good market on their own merits. This is especially true of every man who is conscientious in regard to the interest of his employer. It seems to be the aim of labor organizations to make the laborer as inefficient and impotent as possible. It is a levelling process, and any special energy or enterprise is discountenanced. A man who displays these qualities is on the road to independence; therefore, he receives no encouragement. It is assumed that labor is a curse, and the less of it that one can get along with, the better. The theory is, that with fewer hours, or a smaller amount accomplished, the more room will be left for the employment of others of the organization. It requires but a glance at these well-defined tendencies to see that they do not conduce to the formation of any type of character that is manly or self-reliant. The sentimentality of the times that looks upon the working man as a poor, oppressed, downtrodden being, is absurd when applied to an American laborer, and his self-respect ought to rebel against any such assumption.

The theory that wages are worth such a sum, regardless of the market, is not sound; and every workman of any intelligence ought to be able to see it. There is no other possible conclusion in harmony with Natural Law, but that a thing is worth what it will bring in a free and untrammelled market. The benevolent idea that wages should yield a fair support has no application in the business world. Charity is the highest and brightest of all virtues in its proper sphere; but its province is not in fixing market prices. The charitable idea would not harmonize with the dignity of labor, and every intelligent and self-respecting laborer would scorn the sentiment that he is a pauper or semi-pauper, or that he ought to receive what he had not fairly earned. No; the average working man of America is well able to take care of himself, and is not so imbecile as to require guardianship. It is for him to decide whether it is for his interest to accept an offer for his services, or to look further for a better market. He is a man; and, as such, should do business upon business principles. As a man, he should strive to escape a condition of dependence, and to become an independent member of society.

Third. Personal freedom of action and contract is surrendered to the control of others, whose judgment is often faulty and prejudiced.

The question comes to every intelligent workman: Can I afford to surrender my personal liberty, freedom of choice, duties to myself, family, and conscience, to any secret and irresponsible tribunal? Can I consent to be ordered "out" or "in," regardless of my personal wishes, in a land where personal liberty of action is the distinguishing characteristic?

With perhaps the exception of the society known as the "Brotherhood of Locomotive Engineers," which is more especially a benevolent organization, the system of strikes seems to be an important element in the working policy of labor combinations. Strikes are violent efforts to defy Natural Law, and are, therefore, harmful and expensive. Even when apparently successful, it will be found that their influence, in the long run, is not advantageous.

The most conservative and moderate estimate of the direct loss to the laboring men of the United States, caused by the strikes of the year 1886, would mount high up in the millions, and their indirect results, if their influences could all be traced out, would be found to be even greater. The discharge of a single union man, or the retention of a single non-unionist, has been made the excuse for a strike involving thousands, with all its attendant suffering and expense. All this to vindicate a supposed principle, which really turns out to be only a sentimental "boomerang." Such was the nature of the very extensive and disastrous strike which took place in the spring of 1886, on what is known as the Gould system of railroads, extending from St. Louis to Texas. Thousands of men, many of whom had families depending upon their daily earnings, were "ordered out" of good situations, which they never afterwards regained. Thousands of others, whose business was more or less directly connected with these men, were thrown out of employment, and business of all kinds was largely interrupted for weeks in three or four States, causing great loss to all classes. Much property was destroyed, and many non-union workers were injured and maltreated. All these, and other ills too numerous to be mentioned in detail, resulted from the ill-advised and cruel orders given to confiding working men by labor officials. It seems to be a fact beyond doubt, that what would have been a great and general resumption of prosperity in the business of the whole country, which had begun to set in strongly in the early spring of 1886, was not only postponed, but almost destroyed, by the labor disturbances which came like an epidemic in April and May of that year. And furthermore, these troubles did not appear to be spontaneous in their character, but they were "ordered," engineered, and fomented by agitators, who did not belong in the ranks of the working men. If things had remained in their normal and peaceful condition, so that the era of general prosperity had really got under way, the increased demand for labor would have caused a natural advance in wages, as has always been the case, and general prosperity so long desired would have come to remain. One more example of "killing the goose that lays the golden egg." Natural Law is a most powerful and serviceable friend, but if we will persist in making it our enemy, we must reap the consequences. The disastrous effects of the gigantic labor disturbances in Chicago, during April and May, 1886, are still fresh in mind. The general suspension of business, and the disorganized condition of things in that city, gave the Anarchists their long-looked-for opportunity to begin their warfare on society. To the great credit of laboring men, they, as a rule, condemn many things that are proposed to be done in their name. The Anarchists, and other enemies of society in general, are not found to any extent among laboring men. They despise labor and the laboring man, but at the same time try to make him their tool. One or two more instances of the effect of strikes will suffice, for they are all very uniform in their results. In July, 1886, a large number of tanners, employed in the extensive establishments of Salem and Peabody, Mass., were "ordered out." In the end, most of the men lost their places, and had to remove elsewhere to find work. During several months, assaults, intimidation, and disorder continued more or less, and the towns were put to large extra expense to protect, as well as possible, those who wished to work. The indirect losses and suffering growing out of this strike can never be estimated. The Peabody *Reporter* made a very careful estimate of the direct results on Nov. 10, 1886. A personal canvass of all the shops of Salem and Peabody was made, and every detail carefully ascertained. It gives the result as follows : —

"On July 12, 1,500 men left work in forty-three factories, and on November 10 there were employed in these same factories 1,205 men. In the other thirty-one factories, 613 men went out at the same time, and in these factories 509 men are now at work. This makes a total of 2,113 men who quit work July 12, and a total of 1,714 men employed in the same factories to-day. Had these men worked, they would have received $456,408. It is estimated that they have lost, aside from the amount received from the **Knights of Labor**, $304,272."

As a result of the eight-hour agitation during the spring and summer of 1886, the pork and beef packers of Chicago gave that system a continued and thorough trial. As competing cities continued on the ten-hour basis, the inevitable result soon became apparent. The business could be done more cheaply at those places, and, as Natural Law is inexorable, the business was rapidly transferred to them. The Chicago packers, finding it useless to hold out against the inevitable, notified their help early in November that they would be obliged to return to the ten-hour system. Rather than accede to this, nearly twenty thousand men were "ordered out"; this, just at the beginning of winter, when the great majority had nothing ahead, and thousands of them had families dependent for subsistence on their daily labor. The hostile presence of such a mass made it utterly unsafe and impracticable for any minority to continue at work. The very few that attempted to do so found that their lives and homes were in imminent danger. Plenty of non-union men, who wanted to work, could only be protected by the use of two regiments of infantry, sent at the expense of the State, in addition to large numbers of private police. It is true that officials of the Knights of Labor discourage violence, but the difficulty is with the system. It is a cruel thing to order twenty thousand dependent and unintelligent laborers out of their positions at the beginning of winter. It is folly to expect that they will stand idly by and see their places taken by others. It is easy to say to them, "Keep quiet," but these unfortunate men have a terrible pressure on them, forcing them *not* to keep quiet.

Let us look for a moment at the ultimate effect of a rise in wages, when caused by the successful efforts of labor organizations, in a quiet manner and without striking. For illustration: Suppose that the natural and competitive cost of a certain style of boot is $5.00 per pair, as produced in Massachusetts manufacturing towns, and that 100,000 pairs are made and sold annually. Now suppose that the labor unions in the city of Lynn get such a thorough control that by quiet pressure, the crimper, laster, stitcher, and the various other kinds of workmen each establish a moderate advance, so that it now makes the cost of the boot $5.25, instead of $5.00, as before. The combination here have carried their point, but let us see if they have made any gain. The first effect would be seen in a lessened demand. The average man would wear his old boots a little longer, or would buy some other style in place of them. Instead of 100,000 pairs, it would be found at the end of the year that a less number, say 90,000 pairs, had been the limit of demand. Therefore one tenth of these workmen have been thrown out of employment. Now look at another effect.

If in Haverhill, and other competing points, natural competition still enables the same boot to be produced for $5.00, the business would at once begin to leave Lynn; for, by Natural Law, it always seeks the cheapest producing points. So that not only the general demand would fall off, but competition would soon force the Lynn manufacturers to stop entirely the production of this boot. Some of the workmen of Lynn would have to sacrifice their homes, and move elsewhere, and the place would run down. Some one may reply that by general combination, the advance could be obtained at all points in the State. That would not in the least affect the first result, which was a lessening of the general demand. But, in addition, if all the State combined, it would tend to drive the business to other States, and to the West and other parts of the country. This would cause a loss of dollars to the Massachusetts boot makers, in an attempt to grasp dimes. With the levelling influence of world-wide competition, such an artificial attempt is worse than useless. It is harmful. The principle illustrated in the case of boot manufacturing is universal in its application, and no kind of production is exempt from its irresistible control. A man might as well try to lift himself by the straps, when wearing one of these pairs of boots, as to expect to mount above the force of these fundamental business principles, or to escape their penalties.

If it were possible by universal combination among working men to advance wages fifty per cent, it would not in the least improve their condition. The price of everything they need would be enhanced in the same proportion, and they would have no larger surplus at the end of the year than before.

The system of assessments necessary to keep in motion all the machinery of labor organizations, including the salaries of officials, together with the very large sums necessary to maintain in idleness those who are "out," adds still more to the burdens of the working man. War is always expensive, and this conflict, not with employers, but with supply and demand, is a costly operation. The promises made by the labor agitators seem attractive and desirable, but their fruits will be found bitter. It is noticeable that vehement champions of the labor cause, who have been zealous to have the assumed wrongs of the working man righted, have, in many cases, soon after been found in the field as candidates for some political office. In the spring of 1886, the chief officer of the

Knights of Labor issued a very emphatic warning to the members of that organization to keep out of politics, suggesting that the success of the movement depended upon their following the course advised. In a few months from that time, however, we find the organization active in the political world, and casting a solid vote for a socialistic agitator for the mayoralty of the leading city of the Union.

When sentimental socialists try to make the working man dissatisfied with his condition, by teaching him that labor is a dependent condition, and that he is in slavery, the laborer should not forget that the average price of labor has for many years been steadily advancing from natural causes. The price of labor is now about double what it was thirty or thirty-five years ago. On an average, it took double the amount of labor to buy a given amount of flour, sugar, clothing, and most other necessities, that it does at the present time. The single item of rent is probably dearer, but, with that exception, nearly everything used by a laboring man has declined during the period in which wages have doubled. This shows a real and great advance in labor values from the operation of Natural Law, and would probably be still higher than it is at present, had it not been obstructed and hindered by the active operations of labor unions during the last two years. In spite of the influence of unrestricted immigration, the rate of wages with us is, in general, more than double what it is in Europe. Everything seems to show that the present unrest, now existing among the manual laborers of America, is in no degree the result of recent changed conditions for the worse; but that it is entirely due to the sickly sentimentalism and semi-socialistic doctrines, the seeds of which are so persistently sown by foreign agitators, and whose theories are so abundantly advertised by the sensational portion of the newspaper press. The vagaries of the greatest extremists thus get a very large amount of notoriety.

In regard to boycotts, we shall only observe that they are unbusinesslike and revengeful in their conception, unnatural and un-American in their methods, and deranging in their effect on all legitimate business. It is a privilege and a necessity for the wage-worker who has limited means to expend, to buy the best goods at the lowest prices possible in a free market, whether they were made by union hands or not. To pay more for purposes of revenge is a loss to the laborer, and an injury to society, of which he is a part.

Fourth. They are tyrannical in their action towards all unorganized laborers.

They assume to represent labor in general, but statistics show that but a small part of the grand aggregate of laboring men belong to organizations. The interests of this great mass of unorganized men are, to a great extent, ignored by the public and despised by the combinations. No matter how honest, industrious, and law-abiding they may be, they are "scabs," and they often receive a moral, and sometimes a physical treatment more worthy of criminals than law-abiding men. The public, with a singular absence of that sense of justice which is supposed to be dear to American citizens, apparently expect more or less of this condition of things as a matter of course, and moral and social abuse and opprobrium, when not accompanied by physical assault, is treated as a matter of slight consequence. Human law professes to protect every man in the right to either buy or sell labor or other commodity in the open market. A recent writer has well said that, "Attempts to do away with this right by force, intimidation, or interference have their logical end in anarchy. The majesty of the law is the foundation of all our liberty and prosperity, and every man should give it his moral support."

The sentimental writers, as a rule, utterly ignore this unorganized majority of laborers, as though no such people existed. When they speak of labor, they only refer to the minority portion, or that which is organized. Are not these men American citizens, and are they not entitled to common rights and protection, under a form of government which professes to be democratic and impartial? They have a right to sell their labor as they choose to willing purchasers, and when the government fails to protect them in this right, then American boasted freedom and liberty is a sham and a farce. These men, as a class, are ignored by the politician in his zeal to bid for the labor vote, and even the newspaper press, as a rule, gives them scanty recognition. They are quiet, peaceable, law-abiding, and not obtrusive or loud; but, at the same time, they form a very solid and important part of the live-oak in the hull of the "Ship of State."

Fifth. Their logical tendency and influence is in the direction of socialism.

Socialism as a system will be discussed in a separate chapter, but the logical tendencies that have cropped out of the agitations of organized labor are so marked, that it is proper to note them briefly in this connection. When natural and business principles are left behind, and sentimental methods are adopted, all solid ground is abandoned. As well attempt to found a solid structure on the quicksand, or combine mathematics with fiction, as to expect that the current of business can run smoothly in an obstructed channel. The natural and logical outcome of any compulsory kind of socialism in the end, is the disruption of society and government. When the anchor is hauled on board of a craft which floats on the bosom of a river, it naturally drifts down stream. Any candid man must have observed that there is, and has been, a close sympathy between labor and social organizations, especially in the larger cities. The socialist holds out an alluring bait to the ignorant masses of foreign laborers, and soon they are made to feel that, because some others have more of accumulated labor than they have, the world has not been fair with them, and that they have not had their rights. Labor combinations and socialism shade into each other, and it is natural that they should, for socialism is nothing more nor less than logically advanced sentimentalism. As before noticed, the followers of Henry George find an encouragement in the solid vote of organized labor, and the great moral pressure brought to bear upon every member in New York to vote for him does not well comport with the idea of a free ballot. Any candid, unprejudiced view of the situation discloses the fact that labor organizations are drifting toward dangerous ground.

Let no one claim that the foregoing chapter is directed against labor, for it is most decidedly in its interest. Natural Law, when respected, freely offers its benediction and aid in behalf of all honest labor and industry. The welfare of labor is the welfare of society.

This study of labor organizations has been made from the laborer's standpoint and in his interest. We believe that truth is the best friend of the working man, and that error and prejudice are his worst enemies. It is a great misfortune to laboring men that they so often mistake false friends for true ones.

SOCIALISM.

"Where law ends tyranny begins."

Wm. Pitt.

"Of what avail the plough and sail,
  Or land or life, if freedom fail?"

"Vice is a monster of so frightful mien,
  As to be hated needs but to be seen;
  But seen too oft, familiar with her face,
  We first endure, then pity, then embrace."

Pope.

V.

SOCIALISM.

IT is only necessary to make an application of the principles of Natural Law to socialistic systems, real and proposed, to find that they are not adapted to man's constitution. They are, therefore, artificial and impracticable. If they are unnatural, it follows necessarily that they are harmful and destructive. Their naturalness is the true test, and if that is wanting, it becomes certain that their wide or general application to society can never be successful or beneficial. Webster defines socialism as "a social state in which there is a community of property among all the citizens." It is foreign to our purpose to attempt any historical or detailed study of the various societies or organizations that belong to this general class. Though differing widely in theory and doctrine, they have certain features in common, and these are visionary and abnormal in their character. In their practical destructive effects on society they are quite unlike; for while the milder forms of voluntary socialistic communities may be harmless, the more violent and compulsory kinds, if carried out, would result in social chaos. Socialism is not indigenous to American soil, and is an exotic in any country where free and constitutional government prevails, for its assumed merit is that it is the opposite of despotism. As by Natural Law extremes meet, so violent or compulsory socialism becomes itself despotism. Its apostles and advocates in this country are rarely found among native American citizens, or even among those of foreign birth who have any intelligent appreciation of our political system. There are at present in the United States three distinct socialistic organizations, whose avowed purpose and aim is a social revolution. Two of these advocate its accomplishment by violent warfare and the destruction of property, so that there is apparently no real distinction between them and the avowed Anarchists. They are willing to engulf society, themselves included, in general ruin, and to relapse into consequent barbarism, rather than that existing civilization and government should continue. That these extremists gather moral encouragement from milder socialists, some of whom advocate the same end, but hope to bring it about by peaceful means, is beyond a doubt. The pronounced sentimentalism of the times, which is making such efforts to set aside natural principles, is, though perhaps unwittingly, lending encouragement in the same direction. The warfare against Natural Law is carried on by an army of allies whose several motives and aims greatly vary, but in this general hostility they are a unit.

Experience, which is the indorser of law, shows the uniform failure of socialism as a system, even when tested by experiments under conditions most favorable to success. Voluntary socialism, in limited communities, under the most flattering circumstances, and with the most conscientious and enthusiastic leaders, has been tried again and again, but with little success. It is true that in certain instances societies having socialistic features have existed for some time, but in none has this characteristic been one of vitality and growth. Where they have not entirely disintegrated, they have led a lingering existence in spite of more or less communistic ideas that found place in their systems. If such mild, harmless, and promising experiments have proved futile, what might be expected as the result of a violent and compulsory commune, attempted, not with a voluntary and picked community, but with all the heterogeneous elements of society? A menagerie let loose would be a fit illustration of the result. It would very likely produce an upheaval similar to the French Revolution. World-wide experience, as well as the teachings of Natural Law, proves the truth of the proposition: *That the condition of civilization or barbarism among nations is in proportion to the security and inviolability of individual property rights.* Adam Smith asserted that the security afforded to property by the laws of England had more than counterbalanced the repeated faults and blunders of the government. It is not too much to claim that the foremost and commanding position of England and the United States among the nations of the earth is due to the safeguards erected around property rights, and the but slightly obstructed operation of natural laws by governmental or other interference. No nation can be named where property rights are insecure, in which there is not a coexisting state of barbarism. These truths are so obvious that it seems superfluous to demonstrate them. But the fact remains that charlatans in political economy are making great efforts to disseminate opposite theories, and apparently with much success. In this they are aided by the sensational portion of the newspaper press.

It is the main province of legislation and political science to provide the best and surest means for protecting property rights. This is all-important, for the reason that the right of property is the most powerful of all encouragements to industry and the increase of wealth. *The certainty that a man can enjoy the fruits of his toil is the stimulus to all production, enterprise, and prosperity, with the individual and nation.* In those parts of the world where the title to property depends upon a strong right arm, or where it is liable to be confiscated by the ruling power, production is confined to its rudest and most primitive forms. Henry George's doctrine of general or governmental ownership of land is already in force in parts of Asia and Africa, and, as a natural result, there is no fixed property except of the rudest description, and valuables are either hid in the earth, or quickly carried by caravans to places where private ownership is recognized and protected. This plausible writer proposes by the adoption of his plans to do away with poverty, and he begins with the confiscation of all private property in land. He would take the house-lot of every man who has been thrifty enough to acquire one, but would graciously permit the owner to retain the building. But with increased pressure from a naturally enlarged class of the unthrifty and improvident, it seems probable that the next step in order would be to take the house also. After leaving the firm anchorage of perfect security to property afforded by government and law, there is no solid ground along the route before the end is reached, which is the denial of all right. From the very nature of the case, there is no middle ground. In the opening of Chapter III., Book VII., of "Progress and Poverty," the author says: —

"The truth is, and from this truth there can be no escape, that there is, and can be, no just title to an exclusive possession of the soil, and that private property in land is a bold, bare, enormous wrong, like that of chattel slavery."

And further on in the same chapter: —

"And by the time the people of any such country as England or the United States are sufficiently aroused to the injustice and disadvantages of individual ownership of land to induce them to attempt its nationalization, they will be sufficiently aroused to nationalize it in a much more direct and easy way than by purchase. They will not trouble themselves about compensating the proprietors of land."

Nationalization has a softer sound than forcible seizure or robbery, but in this case it evidently means the same thing. The crime would be the same whether it was committed by the government or by armed outlaws. With such a starting point, this writer evolves from his own imagination a Utopian condition of society in which the present ills are nearly or quite all eliminated. What a marvellous edifice for such a foundation! Reference is made to this work on account of the notoriety of its author, and its very wide circulation. Its unique boldness and audacity have given it a greater amount of free advertising than has been bestowed on any ten useful and practical books that have been issued during the last five years. Its sentiments and conclusions remind one of the fanciful dreams of an opium-eater, full of beauty, color, and harmony, but whose realization is grim, black, and hideous.

With human nature as it is, how many would be provident, industrious, or economical under the most perfect system of socialism yet conceived? Enterprise, ambition, invention, and progress would all wither, as if under the shade of the deadly upas. If an ideal millennium had come upon the earth, so that men loved others more than themselves, there would be but little use for civil law or government. Until such a time, and until self-interest shall cease to be the main-spring of human action, they will be indispensable to define and protect individual rights.

The genius of socialism seems to be embodied in the old adage that "the world owes every man a living." No matter how lazy, improvident, or reckless he may be, his industrious neighbor, who by patient toil has become the owner of accumulated labor, is expected to divide with him, and, in future, to keep on dividing.

Socialistic agitators ring so many changes on such recently coined phrases as "impending revolution," "wage-system slavery," "industrial crisis," etc., indicating some expected revolution, that many poor dupes actually look for a time not far distant when the government will invite them to help themselves to their neighbors' land and goods, and when work will be a thing of the past. Is it a wonder that great masses of ignorant emigrants become saturated with such ideas, when it is considered that socialistic, atheistic, and anarchic literature is their chief intellectual diet? Many are not aware of the extent to which this condition of things exists among the great number of Poles, Bohemians, and the lower class of Germans, who are found in solid masses in all our large

Western cities, and who know little or nothing of our institutions or language. Here is a fertile field for sowing the seed of moral and economic truth. The right sort of books in their own tongues would do much to neutralize the baneful influences which loom up like a black cloud on our national horizon.

DEPENDENCE AND POVERTY.

"*Teach every man to spurn the rage of gain;
Teach him that states of native strength possess'd,
Though very poor, may still be very bless'd.*"

Goldsmith.

"*To a close-shorn sheep God gives wind by measure.*"

"*Help thyself and God will help thee.*"

Herbert.

VI.

DEPENDENCE AND POVERTY.

THE charitable societies and organizations of the city of London are far more numerous and wealthy than those of any other city in the world, and in no other place is there such a vast amount of abject and hopeless poverty. What relation have these two facts to each other; or, in other words, which is the cause and which is the effect? If we study human nature in the light of Natural Law for the solution of this problem, and also carefully observe the teaching of experience, we shall find that supply and demand equal each other here, as in the domain of commerce. Let the supplies of charity be doubled or quadrupled, and the demand from dependence will keep pace with it. These relations and sequences being general and uniform, prove that they are not a matter of chance or uncertainty, but, rather, are governed by natural and unvarying principles. As rapidly as dependence can find something to depend upon, it will multiply and increase. In contrast with London is Paris, where race, conditions and customs would lead us to expect more and worse poverty. We find instead much less, and of a less hopeless variety. Paris makes but a small showing in charitable organizations when compared with London, where the variety and number of old, wealthy, and thoroughly organized and equipped benevolent associations is remarkable. These illustrations and similar ones, which might be cited, do not prove that charity is an evil. It is *misapplied* charity, which is not truly charity at all, of which the world has been full, that is out of harmony with natural principles.

Charity is divine, heaven-born, and the brightest and noblest of all virtues; but this does not alter the fact that so-called charity, misapplied, breeds dependence with unerring certainty.

The diseased, aged, helpless, and impotent are within its sphere, and he who has surplus wealth gets the most real sweetness out of it by applying it directly to lessen the misery and lighten the burdens of this ever-present class. Natural Law is not uncharitable, or cold and mechanical, as some might hastily conclude; but is compassionate and bountiful, whenever it is not transgressed and defied. Benevolence is normal, and the hospitals, asylums, and other humane institutions are not only entitled to our merciful regard, but we owe them a debt. Charity is a natural quality, and it would be unnatural not to exercise it. It is, perhaps, fortunate for society that it has its helpless and really dependent class, for it furnishes an ample field for the exercise of the kindly and brotherly motives of man's nature. While all these facts cannot be too greatly emphasized, it remains that every man who has in him the possibilities of independence, is degraded and injured by opportunities to lean upon anything outside of himself. The contrast is the widest possible between the results of charity exercised in its true sphere, and those of its abuse, or when applied outside of its legitimate functions.

The so-called paternal governments of Europe have in them elements which tend directly to add to the numbers and degradation of the dependent classes, and to make their condition more hopeless and fixed in its character. It is just as demoralizing and destructive of a self-reliant manhood to lean upon the State, as upon some private organization. A government that upholds the rule of *laisser faire*, or non-interference, is that under which true manhood and independence are developed and cultivated.

Mrs. James T. Fields, in her admirable book, "How to help the Poor," says: —

"To teach the poor how to use even the small share of goods and talents intrusted to them proves to be almost the only true help of a worldly sort which it is possible to give them. Other gifts, through the long ages tried and found wanting, we must have done with. Nearly a million of dollars, in public and private charities, have been given away in one year in Boston alone; and this large sum has brought, by way of return, a more fixed body of persons who live upon the expectation of public assistance, and whose degradation becomes daily deeper. The truth has been made clear to us that expenditure of money and goods alone does not alleviate poverty."

A sharp line of demarcation needs to be drawn between a poor man and a pauper. There is little necessary resemblance between poverty and pauperism. It is the worst calamity that can befall a poor man to become pauperized. He who blindly scatters money in the name of charity is liable to do incalculable harm. On the other hand, he who teaches a man how to help himself, and raises him from the dependent into the thrifty class, does society and humanity a great favor. No person of means can discharge his obligations to society by careless and indiscriminate giving. Industrial schools, and any other aids that teach the way of self-support, and give the young such a training as will put them on their feet, deserve the most liberal support and encouragement. Help some dependant to discover a path of self-support, for by this act of real charity you bring him into harmony with Natural Law, and no gift of money could equal that favor. The knowledge of something to fall back upon in the future, outside of one's own exertion, causes improvidence in the present. The tramp who knows that charity and the soup-house are in readiness for him when winter comes, will not put forth much effort to find employment during the summer and autumn.

It is not the province of this book to present statistics to prove how much the dependent and pauperized classes are increased by intemperance, vice, and crime. That these are the true causes, however, of nine tenths of the poverty, misery, and degradation is evident to any candid observer. It is idle and fallacious to attribute evils due to these causes, to any inherent fault of our present social system.

EMPLOYERS AND THEIR DUTIES.

> *"And each shall care for other,*
> *And each to each shall bend,*
> *To the poor a noble brother,*
> *To the good an equal friend."*
>
> — *Emerson.*

> *"Why should a man whose blood is warm within,*
> *Sit like his grandsire cut in alabaster?"*
>
> — *Shakespeare, Merchant of Venice, Act I.*

> *"And learn the luxury of doing good."*
>
> — *Goldsmith.*

VII.

EMPLOYERS AND THEIR DUTIES.

NATURAL Law has some plain words for employers, for they, no less than employés, are under its dominion, and, if transgressors, are subject to its penalties. While business should always be done on business principles, there is abundant room and opportunity for other obligations outside of that of service rendered and paid for. Natural Law comprehends within its scope not only economic and mathematical business rules and methods, but it provides an important place for the exercise of the kindly and brotherly elements that are inherent in man's nature. These, while not strictly entering into business itself, surround, gild, and refine it, lighten its burdens and soften its cares. They are like the springs and cushions to a carriage, which, while they have no direct relation to the speed or distance, render our progress much more comfortable and easy. Natural Law is democratic. It recognizes a man as a *man* as long as he fulfils the conditions of manhood. The duties of an employer to his workmen are entirely discharged with the payment of stipulated wages, so far as they stand related within the business and economic sphere; but there are other relations that cannot be ignored. They involve a recognition of the fact of man's brotherhood, and that he is a part of one moral and social economy; and these relations, though different, are equally natural and necessary. As harmony with Natural Law always lends powerful aid in the direction of success, the employer who gives heed to these higher and finer claims upon him, not only better discharges his obligation to society, but at the same time smooths the road toward his own prosperity and reward.

Employers should not forget that the employed are men, not machines. A larger kindliness toward and interest in employés would largely dispel that illusion of a natural antagonism, on which labor unions flourish and production decreases. The workmen are the staff of the employer. A general might almost as well expect a successful campaign with his staff selected from the hostile army, as for an employer to expect good, honest service from men whose feelings are antagonistic, whether with, or without, good cause. Cultivate friendliness and sympathy with your employés, not by flattery and smooth words, but by genuine interest in their welfare. The great difficulty, especially in large establishments, is that employer and employed are too far apart. There is little or no personal contact or community of feeling. Misunderstandings and difficulties vanish when discussed face to face in a kindly spirit. Show your employés that you are more truly their friend than is the labor agitator, who comes from the outside to stir up strife, and his occupation will be gone. In this direction, and this only, can be found the remedy for labor troubles, and the only solution of the so-called labor problem. Disband the horizontal and combative combinations of laborers with laborers, and employers with employers, and cultivate alliances and interests in the other direction. This would have to begin with some conciliation on both sides, for both have been looking in the wrong direction, and moving on the wrong track. The pecuniary success of both parties can only be increased by this means. This change of front is very important, notwithstanding it is in direct opposition to the ground taken by many recent eminent writers on the "labor problem," the burden of whose works has been to urge working men into combinations hostile to their own interests. This course will never solve the labor problem, but will render its solution more difficult. The head and hands must have one object, or else there will be trouble for both. Let the employer also bear in mind that all that has been recommended on his part he can do without injuring either the independence or self-respect of himself or his employé. A unity of interest between employer and employed is natural, because there is no competition between them. *Competition is always horizontal*, or on the same plane. The natural competition of employés is with employés, and of employers with employers. The union should be between the two unlike elements; then each supplements the other and forms completeness. Solidify and strengthen one of these to the utmost extent, to the neglect of the other, and the result is as defective and useless as the sharpening of one blade of a pair of shears with its companion missing.

The best employers naturally attract the best help, and such a combination has great strength. The employer has on his side the risks and contingencies of the business, and therefore, if he is wise, will recognize and cultivate all those elements which tend to harmony, and as a natural consequence, to success. Suppose that after inventories have been taken at the end of a prosperous year, the owner should distribute a certain part of the surplus to his faithful help, does not every one believe that, even from a business standpoint, it would be a good investment? While not a legal obligation, neither would it be a charity, but merely a special reward for special faithfulness. Can we doubt that such a course would be mutually beneficial in the long run? It would take very strong inducements to start a strike among workmen who were dealt with in such a spirit. We have a notable example of this in the case of Leclair, a French employer, who began this system over forty years ago. After suffering from the effects of discontent, antagonism, and unfriendly suspicion among his men, he resolved to try an experiment. In 1842, after calling together the most faithful of his help, forty-four in number, he threw upon the table a bag of gold containing $2,375, distributing to each his share, averaging over fifty dollars per man. This was an object lesson that had an effect. The change was marked. Distrust was replaced by confidence; and, instead of discontent and unfriendly suspicion, a friendly interest and trust became the rule. When the men found that they had an interest in their employer's prosperity, they became more faithful to every requirement, and performed every duty more carefully and thoroughly. The mutual benefits of this plan at once became so apparent that M. Leclair formally adopted it; and, although he died in 1872, his successors continue the practice. At the present time, nearly two hundred firms in Europe have adopted this plan substantially, varying only in minor details. Quite a large number of American firms, also, have adopted this method, or others which are similar in spirit and practice. Messrs. Lorillard & Co., of New York, recently distributed in one year $16,500 among their help, as a part of surplus profits which they were willing to relinquish to their faithful workmen. The results of the various experiments in this direction have been almost uniformly successful, and in several cases to a marked degree. Aside from the actual pecuniary bonus, which in many cases is small, the kindly spirit of which the act is an indication is powerful in its moral effect. A general exhibition of it among large employers would have a beneficial effect in clarifying the muddled labor question.

The employer should also take a deep interest in the dissemination of correct principles in morals, temperance, and hygiene among his workmen, and by his influence and aid, further all practical movements for their improvement and elevation. Opportunities for this vary much in different places and conditions, but there is room for a great and general advance in these particulars. Large employers, whose establishments are in small factory towns, or in isolated communities, have it especially in their power to accomplish much for the good of their help, without any sacrifice of independence or self-reliance on the part of the workmen. Perhaps the most notable experiment of this kind that has been tried in the United States is in the town of Pullman, near Chicago. As the Pullman Company owned the land from the start, they were able to exercise more perfect control than would often be possible; but still, their plan might be approximated in many cases, and with great benefit. Though several thousand men are employed, no places for the sale of liquors are allowed. This alone secures, in general, a superior class of workmen. The houses for the occupation of the employés are built with careful regard for health and sanitary excellence, and, in addition, are models in their tasteful and modest architectural effect. The water, gas, and sewer systems are of the most approved kind, and owned by the company. A public library, schools, churches, and a suitable place of amusement all receive such aid and oversight from the company as will insure their maintenance and efficiency. The rentals of the workmen's homes are fixed on a very moderate scale, being only sufficient to pay a fair interest on their cost, and other facilities are furnished for economy and comfort in living. While the workmen pay for everything they have, thus preserving their independence, they are able to get the best at low rates. The Pullman experiment has been very successful, and is worthy of imitation.

Many employers mistake their own interests, and add to their difficulties, by an unjust and unnecessary severity toward their employés, and the exercise of an overbearing and tyrannical spirit. If such are prosperous in business, their success is in spite of a formidable obstacle.

A few words in regard to "lock-outs" are in order in this connection. They are artificial and unnatural, and, in many cases, cruel in their effects; and, except in very rare instances to counteract wholesale dictation, they are reprehensible. When they are made for the purpose of artificially forcing down the price of labor, they are to be condemned from a moral point of view; and, in addition, they bring their own legitimate punishment, as a violation of Natural Law. Any kind of combination among employers, having in view a compulsory reduction of wages, or harder conditions, is not only unwise, because it arouses an antagonistic spirit among employés, but is also unprofitable in its after effects. Only in exceptional cases, to resist wholesale tyranny on the part of labor combinations on the principle of combating one evil with another, can there be any excuse for combinations among employers.

What is called black-listing is also a weapon that should be used with extreme care, if at all, because it is very liable to abuse. If it were always confined to bad employés, so proved, it might have redeeming, and perhaps wholesome, features. It is, however, so often employed to gratify personal prejudice, and even revenge, that its legitimate use is extremely restricted.

The natural elements tending powerfully towards success to an employer of labor may be said to be the development of an *esprit du corps* among his help, and the secure possession of their respect, interest, and good-will. An ideal establishment is one where employer and employed are each proud of their connection with the other. Such a combination means the highest wages, and, at the same time, the best and most economical production.

STATE ARBITRATION.

"And sheathed their swords for lack of argument."
 Shakespeare, *King Henry V., Act III., Sc. 1.*

*" Beware
Of entrance to a quarrel; but being in,
Bear't that the opposed may beware of thee."*
 Shakespeare, *Hamlet, Act I., Sc. 3.*

VIII.

STATE ARBITRATION.

THE legislatures of several States have, during the last few years, made provision for boards or tribunals of arbitration, whose business is the settlement of disputes and controversies between employers and employés. These provisions for the machinery of arbitration vary somewhat in detail, but are similar in general plan and operation. As we have only to consider the principle, it is not necessary to notice the various plans for the constitution of the boards, their prescribed rules of procedure, or the limits of their jurisdiction. General experience up to this time confirms the conclusion that no practical or permanent benefits can be expected from arbitration as a State system. It may be of some use in its moral effect, as a temporary expedient or makeshift, to bridge over chasms of active hostility, or for emergencies when reason has lost its sway; but it is useless as a means of the permanent settlement of differences continually arising between capital and labor, while they occupy their present artificial and antagonistic attitude. Courts are already organized, and laws in force, to construe and enforce existing contracts; but the province assumed by these tribunals, at least in some States, of making new contracts between citizens, and of fixing prices other than those established by supply and demand, is a novel and unwarranted advance in the direction of paternal government.

In a recent case in Massachusetts, relating to the rate of wages to be paid by a manufacturing firm to its workmen, a hearing was begun by the State board, upon application of former employés alone (the firm not joining in it), most of whom were elsewhere employed at the time of the application, and some were actually engaged in a competing organization. The firm put in a plea of no jurisdiction. The board reserved the point, but proceeded with the hearing. After several days of deliberation, the board decided not to assume jurisdiction; but the ground of such decision was understood to be the fact that the applicants were not at this time employed by said firm, rather than for the reason that only one side joined in the application. Bearing this point in mind, what manufacturer can possibly have any security in engaging in any business, if he is to be debarred from the natural right and freedom of buying labor at its market price, or at a rate offered by those who are willing to sell? It is evident that no person or corporation will permit the State to transact his business for him; and if the State insists upon so doing, then business must come to an end. As well have a State board to determine the natural or proper market price for potatoes, clothing, or dentistry. Even if this were a proper sphere for this court, it is evident that, in order to arrive at just and intelligent decisions, it must adopt some rules and methods of procedure like a court of equity; that is, it must call in witnesses on both sides, and make up a verdict on the weight of evidence. It is also plain that, even if the State had the right to make arbitrary contracts and prices between citizens, regardless of natural or market values, no board could possibly judge intelligently of the great variety of occupations, conditions, and questions that would come before them. They might be able, intelligent, and honest; but in addition, it would be necessary for them to be universal experts. No two cases would be alike. It would not be simply a question of law and principle, or right and wrong; but, rather, of materials, qualities, markets, credits, competition, expenses, and many other elements that would all have a bearing. Aside, then, from its strained and unnatural jurisdiction, it would be a physical and mental impossibility for any board to grapple with such a variety of problems as would come before them.

Arbitration may have value in its proper sphere, but the fixing of prices and forcing them upon an unwilling purchaser is outside of its legitimate functions. In the construing and enforcing of existing contracts, it is often easier, quicker, less expensive, and more satisfactory than the regular process of law; but its adoption must be voluntary on both sides. The time-honored method of settling disputes by each party choosing one who is familiar with the conditions, and they together choosing the third, the three then acting together to make a just settlement, is a commendable way of adjusting differences without requiring the intervention of a State board.

Conciliation, however, is more feasible, and, in general, more useful than arbitration. There is an important difference between them. The former may be employed, regardless of State law, and is always mutually voluntary. Often all that is necessary to remove serious disputes is the assistance of conciliators who possess the confidence and esteem of both parties. They must also have a thorough knowledge of all the details and peculiarities of the special business, such as would be impossible with any State board. By such means angry feelings and prejudices may often be subdued, and reason and good sense brought to the front. When, in a conciliatory spirit, those who differ can be brought to sit around the same table and reason together in a friendly way, differences rapidly disappear. This would not often be the result of formal arbitration, which has the character of a court of law, in the fact that each side is arrayed against the other. Arbitration, in the proper sense of the word, must proceed under statutory or judicial authority. Even when both parties enter into it voluntarily, they must relinquish their freedom to a great extent by consenting in advance to accept the award of the arbitrators, so as to enable it to be judicially enforced. This gives it essentially the character of a court of law, with all its incidental antagonisms and bitterness. If it has not these features, it is in reality conciliation, and not arbitration.

As long as the present strained and opposing relations exist between capital and labor, disputes and controversies will be numerous and bitter. Any ostensible settlement of them by boards of arbitration will be no more a real settlement than would a truce of fifteen minutes between opposing armies be a treaty of peace. Under the head of conciliation may be included all that is voluntary, friendly, reasonable, and fair in its character, and its possibilities for usefulness are great. Arbitration, which must take account of the legal, opposing, and two-sided phases of a question, is well-nigh valueless for permanent results. There is much of the combative element in human nature, and, instead of stimulating it to greater activity, it should be counteracted and subdued by other qualities which are just as inherent in man's constitution. Only by such means can the different strata of society be united, harmonized, and solidified.

CAN CAPITAL AND LABOR BE HARMONIZED?

"One touch of nature makes the whole world kin."
  Shakespeare, Troilus and Cressida, Act III., Sc. 3.

"He had a face like a benediction."
  Cervantes, Don Quixote, Part I., Book II., Chap. 4.

"Not chaos-like together crush'd and bruis'd,
But, as the world, harmoniously confus'd,
Where order in variety we see,
And where, though all things differ, all agree."
  Pope.

IX.

CAN CAPITAL AND LABOR BE HARMONIZED?

BEFORE considering in the light of Natural Law the direction in which we must look for any improvement in the relations between capital and labor, let us examine the grounds for the present dissatisfaction on the part of the latter. The claim is made on the part of labor that it does not receive a fair share of the profits of production. What constitutes a just division of these products? Exactly what the so-called labor reformers and sentimentalists demand seems to be a matter of great uncertainty. The only unanimity among them is in their dissatisfaction. As any proposed new division must be made by artificial rules, it is not surprising that there can be no substantial agreement. When they abandon the solid ground of natural principles, and embark upon the restless currents of sentimentalism, there is no common resting place.

It is not strange that manual laborers often feel dissatisfied. As a rule, they toil hard for mere subsistence. When they look around and see so many who have not only a sufficiency, but a surplus, they think there must be something wrong in a system under which there is such inequality. But such reasoning is based on a false foundation. Men are created with unequal capacities and powers, and it is beyond human ability to equalize them. Society could as effectually resolve that two and two make five. The world's conclusions already arrived at are in harmony with Natural Law. It values mental force at a higher rate than manual. It would be as futile to expect to change these as to level the Alps. The world is exact and unerring in its estimates. It marks its valuations on both mental and manual force with as great a degree of certainty as coins are stamped in a mint.

The brain force of a McCormick, which conceived the reaping machine, was greater in the results of its production than a million strong right arms which could wield the sickle. The world, therefore, makes its appraisement of his product at millions of dollars, and willingly pays the obligation. The brain power, not only of inventors, but of all those who possess the ability to organize and execute, has a high valuation. The mental force that organizes,

CAN CAPITAL AND LABOR BE HARMONIZED? 121

builds, and puts in operation a great railroad system is worth, perhaps, millions,* because its product may be the settlement and development of two or three States or Territories. If this kind of force were more plentiful, the world would not put such an extravagant valuation upon it. A hundred thousand muscular bodies may be found as often as a single brain of this quality. No amount of sentiment can change the arrangement of these natural principles. Were it in our power to explore beyond the boundaries of human wisdom, we should probably find that it is best as it is. It is only the few who are skilful in originating enterprises and in conducting them to a successful termination. They also have a better knowledge of Natural Law, which they make the most of by securing its aid. If the many could command all these advantages of mental power, there would be a much wider table-land of equality. It is now only the lofty peaks of attainment and production that attract special

* We do not forget that there are men of this class who have amassed large fortunes by stock manipulations which are not a legitimate form of industry. Such an exercise of mental energy is unnatural, perverted, and hostile to the best interests of society. Natural Law would sanction restrictive legislation when applied to such artificial operations.

attention. Having found that inequality is a fixed condition, based on law, it is unwise to complain of it, and foolish to expect to abolish it. Did the Creator make a mistake when he made men of unequal capacity? As it is, every man gets the reward of his own labor. This fact furnishes a continual stimulus to the lower to advance towards the higher. Were it not for brain labor, we should still be in barbarism. It is the increased production of the mental force of the few that has developed civilization. Labor, which is now making the complaint, is getting a large share of the benefits of this improvement. A great share of its blessings is enjoyed even by the humblest.

Capital is only the surplus that is saved above consumption, and it is not only the progenitor of civilization, but it is all that gives value to labor. Without it there would be no such thing as a demand for labor. So far, then, from being envious of another's greater attainment, we should rejoice over it; for we are better off than we otherwise would have been. The capitalist, who, with executive talent and millions of money, has built a railroad, has done a great favor to labor. Boundless acres, before useless, are by its influence transformed into fruitful farms. Thousands of laborers thus find sustenance and occupation, in addition to those who receive direct employment from the railroad. It is a fallacy that the presence of the very rich in society tends to make the masses poorer. It is exactly the opposite. The sentimental and false ideas now prevailing on this subject are the fruit of demagogism and envy. There is a kind of discontent which is wholesome, for it stimulates effort. But the variety now prevailing seems to be of the envious kind, for its spirit is to pull down, rather than build up. If these conclusions are correct, it follows that improvement for labor must be looked for in harmony with them. We shall succeed if we call to our aid the powerful machinery of natural principles, but fail if we challenge and defy them. There is no panacea or charm by which poverty may be abolished, and no rapid cure for the ills of society and inequalities of fortune. There is, however, room for vast improvement, if we seek it in the right direction. We must work along the lines of Natural Law, instead of trying to cross them at right angles.

Before indicating in detail how the relations between capital and labor may be harmonized, let us notice briefly how this desirable result *cannot* be accomplished.

It cannot be done by combinations of like

elements, as of laborers with laborers and employers with employers. Natural competition always exists between those who are on the same level. If, therefore, a number of carpenters organize an artificial combination which holds them together, it is in direct opposition to the law of natural competition, which tends to pull them apart. It is a combination all on one side, and is as incomplete as a carriage would be with two of its four wheels removed. It cannot be accomplished by means of socialistic or paternal forms of government, for the reason that the socialistic principle is fatal to individual enterprise, and antagonistic to all the influences which are necessary to inspire the many to work their way up to the height of the few. Neither can it be brought about by the promulgation of sentimental doctrines which teach the laborer that he is a poor, weak member of society, who needs guardianship. Everything of this kind increases dependence, instead of raising men up to a higher and common level.

Rather should we look for improvement wherever the interests of the two elements can be blended and unified, and production be increased, by subduing prejudice and using conciliation. Promulgate the fact that the interest of one is the interest of both.

Co-operation has been suggested as a solution of labor troubles. This, as a rule, has not worked well. The requisite brain force to organize and conduct business enterprises successfully has generally been wanting among working co-operators. The combined elements lack that variety that is necessary to completeness, and competition soon reveals their deficiencies. In general, these associations do not have the business ability, capital, and other elements of success that warrant the expectation that they will be an important factor in remedying the dissatisfaction of labor.

A system of profit sharing, by means of a more or less intimate industrial partnership, already alluded to, is, however, more promising, and the principle is capable of wide and general application in one form or another. We believe that the escape from present difficulties can only be sought successfully in this direction, for nothing else will weld the two interests that are so popularly supposed to be diverse. The adoption of this plan will require capitalists and employers to take the initiative, which they can well afford to do in view of the prevailing discontent and antagonistic feeling in the ranks of labor. Whether or not there is good foundation for this feeling is not material.

It exists, and therefore some movement must be made, or all interests will suffer. These strained relations result in unwilling, imperfect, and lessened production, causing a loss to both interests. The natural effect on the laborer is seen in his rendering the least possible service that is compatible with full wages. His heart is not in the work. Give him even a small stimulus besides mere wages, and note if there is not improvement. Offer to those who are faithful and industrious a bonus at the end of the year. See if a division in this way of five, ten, or fifteen per cent. of the profits will not prove a good investment. Let the employer be frank with his employés, and thus gain their confidence and respect. In the case of railroad employés, and some other kinds of business, where it is not practicable to divide a percentage of profits, try a system of rewards for faithful and continuous service. The mutual interest in the amount and quality of production is the important feature, and this may be attained in a variety of ways, of which the above are but suggestions. In this way, the employer will have interested friends in his service, instead of inimical laborers working under a temporary truce. This would give to business strength and cohesion. It would be like a pyramid, with the employer at the apex, and beneath, the different varieties of workmen, each supporting the other from the base up. The liability of outside dictation, interference, or strikes, under such conditions, would not be worth mentioning. We earnestly advise employers to try experiments in this direction. It might at first appear that the plans proposed are not strictly in accord with Natural Law; but, upon further trial, we shall find that the union between self-interest and self-exertion is a principle upon which we can surely rely, because it is inwrought in human nature. In social economics, the laws of mind and those of finance must be considered in their connection. They overlap and mingle, and exercise a modifying influence on each other.

A few suggestions to working men in concluding this subject. Even if you have not the promise of a special dividend or bonus, your true interest is with your employer, and not with outsiders. Your hopes of promotion rest with him. As a rule, it will be for his interest to advance you as your merits and services warrant. A half-hearted service has an injurious moral effect on yourself. If you really belong higher than you now are, an opportunity, in accordance with Natural Law, will certainly be afforded you to step up.

ECONOMIC LEGISLATION AND ITS PROPER LIMITS.

" There shall be, in England, seven half-penny loaves sold for a penny: the three-hooped pot shall have ten hoops; and I will make it felony to drink small beer."
    Shakespeare, *King Henry VI.*, Part II., Act IV., Sc. 2.

            " O! it is excellent
To have a giant's strength; but it is tyrannous
To use it like a giant."
    Shakespeare, *Measure for Measure*, Act II., Sc. 2.

X.

ECONOMIC LEGISLATION AND ITS PROPER LIMITS.

TO what extent the State may properly interfere with the industrial freedom of its citizens is a difficult and many-sided question. We shall not attempt to answer it in detail, but rather indicate certain general principles that seem to be deducible from Natural Law, as a guide in its solution. The goal to be reached is the greatest good for the greatest number; and natural principles are the finger-boards that point out the direct route. As a fundamental rule, it may be stated, first, that the State should not interfere in any business or enterprise that may be more economically or efficiently carried on by private control, unless its public character makes it necessary. Second, that it should not interfere in questions of prices, rates, wages, hours, or any others whose proper settlement can only be found in the quotations of a free and untrammelled market.

Under the first of these propositions, let us note the disadvantages of governmental management, as contrasted with that of individuals or corporations. Many examples will occur to the mind of an impartial inquirer, showing the superior excellence and frugality of private over municipal, State, or national administration. The advantage is so apparent, not only in cost, but also in efficiency and thoroughness of management and execution, that it seems superfluous to call attention to it. For example, the public buildings of the United States, built by governmental or political organizations, have, in the aggregate, cost vastly more than if erected under private management. It does not follow that this difference is always the result of dishonesty or mismanagement. It is in the nature of things, or, in other words, in accordance with Natural Law. The more close and direct the connection between the investor and the investment, the greater will be the economy and efficiency; and the more indirect and remote from the contributor or tax-payer the expenditure, the greater will be the waste, mismanagement, and extravagance. It would seem that those persons who are advocating governmental management for our railroads and telegraphs must be blind to these facts, and to the teaching of experience. Take a great railroad system, the successful management of which requires the highest grade of executive talent, and put it under the control of a politician of the dominant party, and the result may easily be imagined. In proportion as the domain of State administration is widened, the amount of "spoils," already too large, is increased, to be fought over under such a plan by politicians every four years. Divorce politics from any industrial enterprise, and a long step is taken in the direction of doing business on business principles. In the face of these undeniable facts, is it not strange that intelligent men urge, with evident sincerity, that the incubus of national and political control be fastened upon some kinds of business now most efficiently conducted by private and corporate administration? It is evident that demagogism is the real foundation of many efforts in this direction. It is expected, as a matter of course, that when a city hall, court house, State house, or custom house is to be built, the expense will be much greater, and the utility much less, than would be the case if the same were done by private enterprise. Official methods are extravagant, and operations under them are so hampered by red tape that they lack directness and efficiency. Rings, combinations, and favoritism are incidental in all such transactions. The opportunity for all these abuses is much greater under our democratic form of government than with the nations of the Old World, whose powers are more centralized. There, the civil service is more a matter of business and less of politics. The necessary sphere of such governmental action among us is limited to those enterprises which, from their public nature, are beyond private control. In general, the rule of *laisser faire* has been the policy of our government in the past, and under it we have greatly prospered. The threatening evil of the present time, however, is an excess of legislation relating to economic subjects.

The second department of detrimental legislation named consists in the efforts to fix prices and rates, which must in the end be inevitably fixed by the law of supply and demand. From a superficial point of view, it might appear that some legislation of this kind would be beneficial, especially as applied to railroads. Whether correctly or not, the courts have decided in favor of the legality of State and national regulation of the rates of freight and passenger service. As this decision must be accepted, the only question remaining is that of expediency. It is urged that railroads are public highways, and that they have special privileges granted by their charters; and for these reasons they should be subject to governmental control. Quite an extensive test of this policy was made, a few years since, by the enactment, in several States, of what were known as "granger laws." Experience has proved that these laws were not only useless, but an injury to the public. It was only another of the oft-repeated attempts to substitute the artificial for the natural. Without State interference, business policy and competition are each constantly forcing the rates for service towards the normal standard, or to such a point as is natural and fair. Take, for instance, the worst supposable case, — that of a road without any apparent competition, either by land or water. The popular estimate of such a road is that it is a "monopoly," and that its policy and interest will naturally cause it to make a tariff of high rates. A more careful examination of the case will show that it is against the true financial policy of even such a road to establish its rates above the normal point. Normal rates attract, foster, and increase both business and profits. Such a road, to be profitable, must adopt a policy that will encourage the location of manufactures, the development of agriculture, and the thorough settlement of the tributary territory. Sagacious railroad managers are learning that a large business at normal rates is far more profitable than a restricted traffic under a high tariff. In other words, they cannot afford to fix rates above the normal any more than below it. It is no doubt true that the managers of some roads have not fully realized the application of this general law; but, as both experience and observation are persistent teachers, the general tendency is strongly in the direction of a normal standard. In numerous instances, roads have voluntarily reduced their rates, thereby realizing as a direct result an increase of business and profits. As equipments and appliances have become more perfect, normal rates have steadily declined, and will continue to do so, regardless of legislation. Every reduction brings a great and unexpected increase of business. The problem before every railroad manager is to find as nearly as possible the normal point; for that, in the end, is the most profitable. In proportion as tariffs are removed from it, either above or below, the profits will decrease. Artificial restrictions prevent the increase of competition and the building of new roads, as some of the "granger States" found to their sorrow, after the adoption of their "cast-iron" regulations.

Some forty or fifty years ago, "assize laws"

were enacted in New York and some other cities, regulating the price and the size or weight of loaves of bread, based on the price of flour. After a trial, which was attended with much trouble and expense, in consequence of the necessity for numerous inspectors, the laws were repealed. Besides the saving of expense, it was found that the natural competition between bakers was much more effectual.

The old usury laws furnish another notable example of attempts to fix artificial prices. As well regulate the height of the tides by statute. When the artificial comes squarely in conflict with the natural, as in this case, the latter will surely triumph sooner or later.

A striking instance of misapplied legislation is seen in statutes to regulate the hours of labor. These have been advocated and urged by so-called labor reformers, and by labor organizations. They have brought a very strong pressure to bear on legislators in favor of these measures. When we look beneath the surface, and see their real effect, we can only be surprised that working men can be so blind to their own interests. Time is the one thing that all share alike. Unlike nearly everything else, the poor have the same amount as the rich. It is, in fact, the capital of the laboring man. By Natural

Law, he has his full time to dispose of as he may think best. But when he asks for an artificial law, which will deprive him of the use of a portion of his own productive power, as by an "eight-hour law," he diminishes by so much his capital, and renders himself poorer. This is the real sum and substance of restrictive legislation, in regard to hours of labor, whenever applied to adults. How unfortunate that American citizens should be so blind to their own interests as to deliberately beg to have their liberty and capital taken from them! If legal enactments are needed to prevent men from selling their time when they wish to, it would logically follow that the State should control their eating and drinking, and what they should wear. It is a reflection upon the intelligence of the masses of the people to suppose that we have any considerable number of adult citizens who are so ignorant that they cannot decide for themselves how much to work. Moreover, even if their physical welfare would be promoted by shorter hours of labor, such legislation would be of no advantage to them unless it were world-wide. If the eight-hour law prevailed in this country, and not in European countries, our manufacturers could not compete with theirs in the markets of the world. More workmen, too, would be attracted to our shores in hopes of an easier time. And both these causes would force down wages.

Legislation in regard to the frequency of payment of wages is clearly superfluous, though, perhaps, harmless except as a precedent.

It is evident that every superfluous and unnecessary enactment decreases the respect for law, and lowers and cheapens the estimation of its justice and impartiality.

The general demand by the masses for the widening of legislative functions, doubtless arises from a vague idea that, by some additional enactments, production would be more equally distributed. For this reason, an effort is made to correct every petty grievance by additional law-making. Prosperity is to be gained by some legal panacea, instead of by the natural road of economy and industry. The present time is prolific in those so-called political economists who advocate new and unique additions to our already cumbersome code. Ignorance of the very first principles of political science can only give rise to such visionary plans and theories. The "reformers" assume that all employers are blindly selfish, and that they try to lengthen hours and depress wages. On the contrary, it is for the interest of every employer to pay good wages and make as short hours as competition and the nature of the business will warrant. Only by such a course can he retain his best help, who are always in demand, and get the highest quality of production.

Business prospers in the absence of legal interference, except to simply provide for justice and freedom.

Bearing in mind the fact, before alluded to, that the expense is much greater when governments, either municipal, State, or national, undertake the accomplishment of any object, even when honestly done, than is the case with individuals, it is obvious that their functions should not be increased except in cases of positive necessity. It is true that the complex arrangements of modern civilization require State intervention in some ways unnecessary under more primitive conditions. The factory legislation of England, and similar enactments in some of our States, are examples. An excess of liberty to some individuals may prove a tyranny to others. As the good of society is more important than the possible advantage of one of its fractional parts, the operations of the few must be restricted when they encroach upon the liberty of the many. In other words, the natural law of liberty, as applied to society, is higher than that pertaining to the individual; and, while they are not in opposition, the lower is modified by the higher. Thus, human law should indorse and supplement Natural Law by restricting personal will, when it conflicts with the will of society. This is compatible with the greatest average freedom for all the different members of the body politic. The primary obligation of the State is in the exercise of what are usually known as police powers. There are a variety of other proper functions which are more or less intimately connected with these primary duties of protection to person and property. We expect the State to enforce our contracts, regulate our sanitary conditions, prevent and punish frauds, abate nuisances, and ward off a variety of evils which threaten society.

Among the examples of factory legislation which may be classed as wise and proper is State interference in behalf of children whose parents or guardians, through motives of cupidity, will not protect them from over-work. The same restrictions in regard to an adult would be superfluous and unwise, for he is responsible, and is supposed to be able to judge correctly as to what is best for himself. Besides, if he is restricted in hours, it might mean for him less food and clothing, and a poorer home. Wholesome regulations relating to fire escapes, sanitary inspection, foul air, the fencing of dangerous machinery and elevator wells, are proper and necessary. They encroach upon no man's liberty, except the liberty to be injured, and private enterprise cannot be relied upon to regulate them. Individual cupidity and neglect must be controlled and overcome by higher supervision. Personal injuries, like libel, slander, or even bodily assault, must be punished by the State, for private punishment would result in disorder and anarchy. Personal will must be subservient to collective will. Individual freedom might lead to the location of a powder mill or glue factory in a thickly settled street, unless it was restrained by collective freedom. It is obviously within the province of the State to appoint boards of health and sanitary inspectors, whose duties shall include the suppression of contagious and epidemic diseases, and the protection of air and water from pollution and contagion. As it is impossible for individuals to be universal experts, it is also necessary to have government inspectors to test weights and measures, to detect adulterations in foods and chemicals, and also, in some cases, to brand those articles of commerce whose quality or quantity cannot be verified by ordinary observation. Organized government has the power to aid and supplement the wisdom of the individual, without in any way restricting his independence, or deadening the competitive and elastic forces of the business world. The boundary lines between State intervention and individual enterprise must, to a certain extent, be determined by a wise expediency; but the great end to be sought is, that private enterprise, activity, and competition shall be left wholly free and unhampered. In the opposite direction lies the great danger of our time. Any unnecessary dependence on the government for objects obtainable by private effort is so clearly a violatian of Natural Law that bad results are sure to follow.

WEALTH, AND ITS UNEQUAL DISTRIBUTION.

" *Order is Heaven's first law; and this confessed,*
Some are, and must be greater than the rest;
More rich, more wise; but who infers from hence,
That such are happier, shocks all common sense."
Pope.

" *He heapeth up riches, and knoweth not who shall gather them.*"
Ps. xxxix. 6.

" *High stations, tumults, but not bliss create,*
None think the great unhappy, but the great."
Young.

" *Man wants but little here below,*
Nor wants that little long."
Goldsmith.

" *A man he was to all the country dear,*
And passing rich with forty pounds a year."
Goldsmith, The Deserted Village.

XI.

WEALTH, AND ITS UNEQUAL DISTRIBUTION.

IT is a very common, but inaccurate saying, that the rich are growing richer, and the poor, poorer. This idea seems to be dominant in the minds of sentimental and socialistic writers, and is largely indorsed by popular opinion. The colossal fortunes that have been accumulated during the last twenty or thirty years attract wide attention, and the conclusion is reached that natural and economic laws are faulty, or else such marked inequality would not exist. Our sentimental preference is for an ideal condition of society in which uniformity is the prominent characteristic. That there has been a great change in the conditions for the rapid accumulation of wealth during the last generation is undoubtedly true. Prominent among the causes which have led to this movement, and which have made the accumulation of great fortunes possible, is the remarkable expansion of our railroad system. The rapidity and extent of our railroad growth are unique, and are unprecedented in the world's history.

Within the last two or three decades, a section of territory larger than the aggregate area of all the States east of the Mississippi River, has been permeated and developed by the construction of these great public highways. The wealth that has been created by this means can only be estimated by thousands of millions. To illustrate this, let us suppose an individual case, and observe the special opportunities afforded for the accumulation of wealth by this great movement. A man with great ability to organize and execute, and with wise forecast, possessed of experience and capital, grasps the boundless possibilities of a sparsely settled and unproductive territory. He foresees that all that is necessary to transform these worthless acres into fruitful farms, and dot them with flourishing towns and villages, is cheap transportation. He projects vast schemes of railroad building, and executes them, not as a philanthropist, but as a sagacious business man. He has faith in natural principles, which show him that the result of his venture will be a domain occupied by thousands of thrifty settlers, who will furnish his road with business. As a result of his energy and persistence, and in strict accord with Natural Law, his individual fortune is, perhaps, increased by millions, and he has earned his reward. Through his instrumentality, there has been added to the capital of the nation, not only the railroad, but many times its value in other products and improvements. Land, before worthless, becomes valuable and productive. Instead of a scanty growth of sage brush, boundless fields of golden grain await the advent of the reaping machine. Where an occasional herd of buffalo was almost the only sign of animal life, numberless droves of cattle and sheep are now seen fattening for shipment, to supply the never-ceasing food demand of the world. In place of vast solitudes broken only by the passing of an emigrant train or Indian hunter, thousands of brawny farmers and laborers find employment and sustenance. This great result is the product of the brain force of one man. He has furnished occupation for thousands of workmen, who otherwise would have been left to overstock the labor market. By the amount of his production he has as fairly earned his millions, as any manual laborer has earned his daily wages. While his own fortune has been enhanced, he has indirectly caused a production many times greater. The transaction was only a sale of brain power, at such a price as the world was willing to pay. The case supposed is only illustrative, but it is typical of many occurring in real life. In the accomplishment of such results, truth is indeed stranger than fiction.

Other important means by which the opportunities for making great fortunes have been multiplied, are found in the utilization of steam and electricity, and by the great number of inventions. These have changed business methods, and increased in almost geometric progression the practical power and possible achievement of a single individual. Great personal ability, when supplemented by such forces, becomes almost irresistible.

The era just past has been a transition period. The remarkable change in business conditions and methods has been so rapid, that comparatively few had the foresight and courage to promptly grasp the golden opportunities as they were presented. They were never so numerous and prolific in any past period, and they furnished the special conditions by means of which, perhaps, nine tenths of the great fortunes have been gathered. Not only the building, but the operating, consolidating, systematizing, and, to some extent, the buying and selling, of these great highways, have contributed to the result. The flow of general capital into small enterprises of a profitable character is easy and rapid, but in great undertakings it becomes timid and suspicious. This has put a very high premium on unusual foresight and executive ability.

The two great estates of Astor and Stewart are instances of great accumulation that have taken place outside of these special conditions and opportunities. They represent respectively the departments of real estate and commerce. The Astor estate furnishes, perhaps, the most conspicuous example in this country of what socialistic writers call "unearned increment." But is there practically any such thing? It is a natural law that any unusual opportunities for gain, will call out seekers and competitors. If the unearned increment is such a prize as we are told, why have not all, or at least more, sagacious men bought land? Simply because they thought there were better investments elsewhere. A careful examination will show that, on an average, a fair interest on the money invested in land, *plus taxes and assessments*, will in the end amount to more than the so-called unearned increment. There are exceptions to this rule in rapidly growing cities and newly settled farming regions, but not more than in other kinds of enterprise. This socialistic bugbear may be disposed of by suggesting that, had there been any greater prospect of profit than in other average investments, the shrewd business men of America would have long ago discovered it, and would have invested more in land and less in other objects and occupations. It is probable that even the Astor estate has paid out in taxes and assessments all the natural increase that has taken place, which *is in excess* of a fair rate of interest on their investments. Land must advance in value very rapidly to outstrip these combined charges. The Stewart estate is an example of what individual brain power, exerted in harmony with Natural Law and by its aid, can accomplish in the domain of commerce and traffic.

The great fortunes that were made in mining, and in mining speculations, belong to an era that culminated several years ago. At present, anything but slow and gradual accumulations in this department is exceptional.

In view of these facts, it seems evident that in most cases the great fortunes were incidental to the unique opportunities presented during the last two or three decades. If these special conditions were temporary in their character, the golden opportunities have largely passed, and fortune making in the future will be slower and more difficult.

In regard to railroad building, nearly all the available territory is now occupied by through or trunk lines, and in future this business will be more confined to the construction of short and comparatively unimportant feeders. The undeveloped territory of our own country is becoming more limited. This will narrow what has been a most prolific field for the rapid enhancement of capital.

It also seems improbable that we can expect any such radical progress in inventions and business methods from the present starting-point, as has been made in the past few decades. Better appliances, and a nearer approach towards perfection in the application of steam and electricity, will no doubt be reached; but unless some new motor, or some means of aerial navigation is discovered, it is impossible to conclude that future improvements will be as radical as those of the last half-century. When a ton of grain can be carried from Chicago to New York for less than it costs to cart it across either city, it is evident that the process cannot be greatly improved.

Again, as wealth has accumulated, the competition of capital with capital has become more intense. Interest, or the selling rate for the use of capital, has declined nearly sixty per cent. It has gradually fallen from the old standard of six per cent. to a point which makes it probable that a two and a half per cent. government bond could be floated at par. If the value of wealth be estimated on the basis of its earning power, a million of dollars is now worth less than one half that amount twenty-five years ago. Competition between investors is so great that almost any railroad, which pays six per cent. dividends on its stock, is in danger of being paralleled.

The general evenness of prices consequent upon telegraphic communication and rapid transportation is another instance of the lessening opportunities for great gains by speculative investments. Important changes in market prices are discounted long in advance, and are, therefore, very gradual. Price fluctuations being smaller, successful corners and manipulations become more difficult and infrequent.

The laws of inheritance are also great and constant forces working toward the disintegration and distribution of great estates. In this country, with no law of primogeniture, and where, as a rule, there are several heirs to each estate, its dissolution as a great unit becomes very probable. The Stewart estate, before alluded to, is an example. The longest life is not sufficient for a single individual to absorb more than a minute fraction of the wealth of the community, and, whether more or less, the probabilities are that at his death it will cease to continue as an organized, accumulative force.

The laws of heredity are also powerful in their wealth-dispersing tendency. While there are exceptions, the sons of very rich men do not commonly inherit the peculiar brain force which characterized their fathers. The dominant and controlling talent is generally greatly modified in the son. Instead of a financier, inclination may lead him to become an artist or a professional man, or still oftener, a gentleman of leisure. In place of the habits acquired by a saving and economical discipline, are those of an extravagant and luxurious character incident to his position. He begins where his father left off; and, in many cases, ends where his father began. Not only the exceptional talent is lacking, in most cases, but the still more necessary impelling motive. Most of our millionaires started in life poor, and were obliged to exercise self-denial and abstinence, which laid the foundation for their future success.

Statistics show that the average life of capital is not equal to the average life of man. It is a prevalent idea that the success which has attended the efforts of the few, is due, in a great degree, to chance or luck, but this is a mistaken view. Favorable environment is important, but exceptional brain power, bringing to its aid the principles of Natural Law, improves and transforms its surroundings. The character of environment, therefore, becomes largely a matter of choice, rather than fixed and uncontrollable.

The general individual average of wealth is higher at present than at any previous time, in consequence of the special causes already enumerated. It also seems probable that the passion for wealth, which has caused so much unfavorable comment by writers of other nationalities, will diminish as conditions become more fixed and opportunities for rapid gain fewer. The fact that the amount of human happiness has but little connection with the amount of wealth possessed by individuals, will become better appreciated. National life and character have hardly had time to become adjusted to the changed conditions brought about by the rapid expansion before noticed.

We have shown that all classes, including the poorest, are greatly benefited by the operations of capital. For illustration, the immense fortunes of Vanderbilt and Jay Gould represent most largely individual wealth in railroads and telegraphs. The fact of personal ownership, with its income of four or five per cent. on the investment, makes no difference with the great balance that goes directly to labor for service and materials. Every laborer gets as much as if the property belonged to ten thousand stockholders, instead of largely to one. This fact also makes no difference with the productive power of capital in performing the multiform functions of society and commerce. If there is a difference in either direction, the organization and operation are usually more perfect under concentrated control. But, aside from these great public enterprises, there are investments of a private nature, and in the domain of art and luxury. The palace of the rich may excite the envy of the passing laborer, but its value in money has already been disbursed to the mechanics who labored in its construction. Every piece of material has been changed, shaped, and fitted from its condition as raw material by busy workmen, who have thereby had occupation and subsistence.

The great and mischievous fallacy which forms the basis of all the socialistic literature and sentiment may be summed up in a single sentence, viz., *that all wealth is created by labor, and, therefore, belongs to the laborers who have produced it.* This plausible proposition, which seems so logical and convincing, may also be disposed of as briefly. The wealth does belong to the labor that produced it, but *the largest and most valuable part of this was mental labor.* The socialists ignore brain labor, which, by Natural Law, is the more important of the two. The large number of clergymen, philanthropists, and benevolent and sentimental people, who have been favorably impressed by some apparently humane and attractive features of socialism, have overlooked this point. The typical European socialist is intelligent and logical. He is a materialist, and does not believe in mind except as being a manifestation of matter. He therefore ignores mind as a factor in production. Even economists of the school of Smith, Mill, and Ricardo, gave little attention to the great part played by brain force in general production. Their observations were made prior to the present era of great invention, when the influence of mental power was not so predominant. The theory that mental effort is not labor, is too shallow to merit serious consideration. Is not the finished edifice as much the work of the architect as of the mason or carpenter? Does not a student, clergyman, merchant, or an inventor labor? On the supposition that wealth is the product of physical labor only, some machines would have a very large value as measured by man power.

Under a government like ours, where all enjoy equal rights, it is a malicious proceeding to foment class feuds and arouse envious passions. It is an abuse of liberty, and its fruit is tyranny.

During the time in which capital has decreased fully sixty per cent. in earning power, there has been an increase in the productiveness of labor. By consulting the tables published by Mr. Edward Atkinson, whose accuracy as a statistician cannot be questioned, we find the following result: In the State of Massachusetts, wages averaged twenty-five per cent. higher in 1885 than in 1860. During the same period, the purchasing power of money, as measured by the prices of two hundred of the most common and necessary articles, also increased twenty-six per cent. This shows that the purchasing power of the laborer's wages is fifty-seven and a half per cent. greater than twenty-five years ago in the State above mentioned, which is probably a fair example in this respect. As the result of an analysis of labor classification, Mr. Atkinson arrives at the conclusion that not more than ten per cent. of all who do the work of the country, intellectual, distributive, and manual, have accumulated an amount of property upon the income of which they can live without personal exertion. In concluding a recent statistical article in the *Century* magazine, he says, "Can it be denied that labor, as distinguished from capital, has been and is securing to its own use an increasing share of an increasing product, or its equivalent in money?"

The aggregate production is much larger, and society richer, by reason of the fact that, in accord with Natural Law, labor is intelligently directed and thoroughly organized by the brain power of capital.

CENTRALIZATION OF BUSINESS.

"All roads lead to Rome."

"For he that hath, to him shall be given."
Mark iv. 25.

"Even there, where merchants most do congregate."
Shakespeare, Merchant of Venice, Act. I., Sc. 3.

XII.

CENTRALIZATION OF BUSINESS.

ANY careful observer, who has watched the currents of trade in the great commercial centres for some years past, could not have failed to notice a constant tendency towards centralization. This movement has been decided and general. It has prevailed not only in American cities and towns, but is also seen in other countries. These facts prove that it is not in consequence of local or special causes, but the result of influences which operate uniformly in obedience to Natural Law. This conclusion is further confirmed by the fact that it has not been caused by, nor in any way connected with legislation. We therefore conclude that it is a necessary feature of the present great development of invention and civilization. There is so much sophistry promulgated at present on the subject of "gigantic and dangerous monopolies," that it is worth while to trace out the working of the natural economic laws which have produced these conditions, and also their legitimate result. This is an era of monopolies. The fact that a few great firms or corporations in each city, and in each department of business, are able to attract a very large and increasing share of the aggregate patronage of the public, is patent to every observer. The Scriptural declaration, that "whosoever hath, to him shall be given," is being literally carried out. For illustration, look at the retail dry-goods trade in any of our large cities. Years ago, this business was done by a large number of small or moderate sized establishments, scattered in different quarters and neighborhoods. At the present time, the great part of this business is done by a few colossal establishments. These great institutions, in many cases, have added building after building, and department after department, until their proportions are of astonishing magnitude. All other departments of trade are more or less under the control of the same natural tendencies. There is also a process of centralization in locality, no less marked. The larger cities, owing to their greater facilities and attractions, and to the ease and rapidity of communication, draw business from the smaller places which was formerly under home control. In addition to this, there is a decided grouping of each kind of business in each city in some special locality. There is a dry-goods quarter, a banking quarter, and one for almost every other leading department of business. Concentration in locality is added to centralization of capital and enterprise.

The operation of this law in connection with manufacturing is also uniform and strong. New industrial centres are formed in conformity with natural conditions and advantages.

Another manifestation of centripetal law is seen in the growth of cities. At distances somewhat uniform, where railroad systems converge, great commercial centres grow up, each having its quota of tributary territory. Their location and growth are not a matter of chance, as many suppose, but are entirely in accordance with fixed laws. When one point gets a fair start in advance of its competitors, like a larger magnet, it has increased drawing power. Its attractive force increases in greater ratio than its growth. It seems to gain a kind of momentum, so that any city of given size has fourfold greater growing qualities than one half as large. While the lesser may increase somewhat, it naturally pays tribute to the greater. This is as irresistible as the law of gravitation. The centralizing force that locates special kinds of business in special places is also well defined. The milling industry of Minneapolis, the packing of Chicago, the importing of New York, are examples. Manufacturing, though not so thoroughly confined to single places, has its focal points: as Pittsburgh in iron, Lowell, Lawrence, and Fall River in cotton, Paterson in silk, and Trenton in pottery.

At first glance, it looks as though this condition of things, especially as relating to great mercantile concerns, was abnormal and injurious. Admitting that it has aspects of this kind, let us carefully examine its results. Imagine a typical American city, with half a million population. Twenty-five years ago, its retail dry-goods business was done by a large number of small shops in different localities. Now it is largely monopolized by half a dozen mammoth establishments located almost side by side. What is the effect of this condition of things on the general public, comprising say four hundred and ninety-five thousand out of the half-million people? They show by their action that (unless they are greatly deceived) they can find lower prices, greater varieties, and better selections at these great establishments than elsewhere. We are obliged to accept this opinion of the great majority of an intelligent public as conclusive. This disposes of ninety-nine hundredths of the entire population. The next class, perhaps five thousand persons, who, under former conditions, would be in business for themselves, are now either junior partners, or employed on salaries by these great firms. They lose the net difference, whatever that may be, between the two following positions: on the one hand, greater independence and the dignity of proprietorship, but accompanied with uncertainty of success; and, on the other, sure, but moderate success, with more dependence. The fact that but a small proportion of men succeed when in business for themselves, as shown by statistics, will still reduce the net difference so much that, even with this small class, it is doubtful which way the advantage would lie. These two classes comprise everybody except the great firms themselves, whose interests it is not necessary to consider. These great institutions have attained their prominent positions by a regular system of evolution, and are fair illustrations of the "survival of the fittest." Given, a rare combination of capital, executive ability and power to organize, with favorable environment, and we have the conditions of increase almost without limit.

In tracing still further the operation of these

laws, let us, for illustration, select two great monopolies, which are, perhaps, popularly regarded as the most obnoxious of any in this country, viz., the Western Union Telegraph Company and the Standard Oil Company. It must be understood that no defence or indorsement is intended of the various means they have used, which have contributed to their present prominence. It is not their private transactions, but their relations to the general public, that we are now considering. No one is forced to have business relations with them, unless he does it of his own free will, and considers it for his interest. It is in their business relation with the public, as sellers of telegraphic facilities and of oil, that we now look at them; for they have no power otherwise to injure the average American citizen. What is now the Western Union Telegraph Company was formed, as nearly every one is aware, by the consolidation of smaller companies and the absorption of rival, but weaker organizations. They were willing and ready to be "absorbed," and were well paid for the operation. The prevalent impression is, that because this business is almost entirely controlled by one great organization, it necessarily becomes a dangerous and powerful monopoly against which the public has no protection. This prejudice against all great corporations is a characteristic of the present time. There may be more danger in the prejudice, or what may come of it, than in the organizations themselves.

Our safety consists in the fact that the natural laws of supply and demand are sovereign, and that there is no danger of their repeal or suspension. What are the practical facts relating to the telegraph company? It is a seller of telegraphic facilities, and the public, which represents demand, holds the key of the situation. The company can afford to sell its services at a lower rate than half a dozen smaller ones could possibly do. Will it? Yes, in the long run; for self-interest will force it in that direction. There is what may be called a normal rate for this service, and, in case the management try to fix prices much above this point, demand falls off and profits shrink with as much certainty as they would in case they were put below it. Managers of corporations do not always discover at once how low normal rates are, and that they are always the most profitable; but experience is a persistent teacher, and these laws are continually pressing in the right direction, until they vindicate themselves and obstructions are removed. An illustration of the operation of natural laws in governing demand, is seen in the effect of successive reductions in the rate of postage. Every experiment made by the government in this way has been successful. The increase of business that followed each reduction was so great, that but a very short time elapsed before the net revenue was larger than before. The true normal rate may still be a little below any point yet reached. Let us examine briefly the other typical monopoly. The business methods of the Standard Oil Company have perhaps received more severe criticism than those of almost any other corporation in the country. But it is difficult to see how even this overgrown giant can injure either the private citizen or the government. It is a colossal producer of oil, but is obliged to go into the open market and sell its product at just what consumers will give for it, and cannot get an eighth of a cent a gallon more than the regular market price. In fact, besides giving employment at good wages to thousands of working men, it is probable that, by use of its great facilities, capital, pipe lines, etc., the millions of consumers are getting oil at a little lower price than would be the case if this admitted monopoly did not exist. It would

CENTRALIZATION OF BUSINESS. 171

seem then, that if this extreme and exaggerated consolidation is powerless for evil, and hedged in by supply and demand, ordinary aggregations of capital are not only harmless, but have their uses and benefits, and are indispensable to society as at present organized.

The fact that railroad or telegraph corporations have, or have not, "watered their stocks," is popularly supposed to have a great influence on their rates of service. Not in the least. If, for any speculative reason, the stock of the Western Union Telegraph Company was largely increased or diminished in its nominal amount, the management would find that it would be entirely inexpedient to change its tariffs for that reason. Its natural facilities would remain as before, and so would the demand for their employment. In other words, the normal point of greatest business and profits would remain the same, regardless of changes in the nominal amount of stock.

We have considered these extreme cases of monopoly, not because we admire or defend them, but only because they furnish another illustration of the supremacy of Natural Law. They may be powerful enough to influence legislation, but they cannot change natural principles. Their business methods, and dealings with rivals and competing organizations may have been indefensible, but unvarying natural conditions will make them powerless to harm the humblest American citizen. They cannot force demand for their products, but only court it.

We are led to conclude that the menace to government and citizens by great business combinations is much overrated. Without regard to legislation, Natural Law hedges them in on every side. Its pressure also against all artificial rings and combinations is steady and strong, and it is with difficulty they can be maintained for any length of time. While great aggregations of capital, in their operations, are subject to many abuses, they are great forces in production, and have an important place in the economic functions of society.

ALTERNATIONS OF PROSPERITY AND DEPRESSION.

" *There is a tide in the affairs of men,*
   Which, taken at the flood, leads on to fortune;
   Omitted, all the voyage of their life
   Is bound in shallows and in miseries.
   On such a full sea are we now afloat;
   And we must take the current when it serves,
   Or lose our ventures."
                    Shakespeare, Julius Cæsar, Act IV., Sc. 3.

" *The time is out of joint."*
                    Hamlet, Act I., Sc. 5.

" *One extreme follows the other."*

" *Every white will have its black,*
   And every sweet its sour."
                    Sir Carline.

XIII.

ALTERNATIONS OF PROSPERITY AND DEPRESSION.

THE course of commerce and trade is very uneven. The alternations of what are popularly known as good times and hard times, are familiar to the most casual observer. Are these recurrences of expansion and contraction, prosperity and panic, governed by fixed laws, or are they largely matters of chance and circumstance? If fixed and unvarying principles control, and have intimate connection with them, any study of such relations cannot fail to be profitable and interesting. The natural law of action and reaction is general in its application, and in no way limited to the business world. The floods of springtime are followed by the droughts of summer. After great activity, comes rest and quiet; after elevation, depression; after light, darkness.

If we soar above the normal business level at one time, we shall certainly fall below it at another; and the higher the flight, the more rapid and great will be the descent. The greatest panics are always preceded by the most intense activity and speculation. These violent changes are disastrous to all industrial interests. Steady and even progress is conducive to solid prosperity, while unhealthful activity is generally deceptive.

What are some of the leading causes and conditions which naturally precede a business climax, and its succeeding panic and stagnation? The fundamental and primary condition which results in panic may be expressed in one word, — debt. In itself, debt is not necessarily an evil, but its abuse is the troublesome element. An experience of profit leads to larger ventures, and these, being successful, to still larger, until both individual and collective indebtedness grows to great proportions. When the crisis comes, all wish for what is due them, and but few are able to pay. Money becomes scarce and abnormally valuable, and productions of every kind unsalable, except at great sacrifice. Business is therefore paralyzed; for all are anxious to sell, and none wish to buy. No human prudence can entirely provide against these convulsions, but a study of their laws and causes may do much to mitigate their severity. A money market always even and in perfect health, would imply the prevalence of an almost infallible wisdom, which is nowhere found.

In times of intense business activity, the fuel is being gathered, stick by stick, and added to the pile which is to produce the coming conflagration. When the conditions are ripe, only a spark is necessary to bring general disaster. The proud fabric which has been gradually rising, and whose stability was unquestioned, is dissolved with appalling suddenness.

The tulip mania in Holland, which occurred in 1636–7, is a striking illustration of the possible intensity of speculation and succeeding panic. A single root was sold for thirteen thousand florins. The ownership of a rare bulb was often divided in shares, and many were sold for future delivery by people who did not possess them, and often when the article sold was not in existence. The crash came without warning, and was most disastrous and complete. The result was not due in any degree to banknote expansion, as Holland at that time had only a coin currency.

Laudable undertakings, if overdone, may issue in panic. The London South Sea Bubble, and some of the railroad panics of America, are examples. They are an evil which no monetary system, however sound, can prevent, and governmental measures are also futile to avert them. With the natural human desire for rapid gain, and convenient facilities for speculation, over-trading is a sure result. It is a peculiar feature that those most actively engaged are less capable of judging of the danger, and the probable time of culmination, than those who look on from the outside. An observer, even in another country, will often discover signs of approaching catastrophe which are overlooked by active participants.

Every important panic is preceded by several years of prosperity, which at length reaches a feverish and unhealthy stage. Industry and economy are at a discount, and slow gains unsatisfactory. Production diminishes as speculation increases. Banks expand their circulation and discounts, and individual and public credits are also enlarged. Confidence is strong, and profits rapid and large. But at length a day of reckoning comes. Some unexpected weak spot in the financial fabric gives way, and every part comes down, as a row of standing bricks are levelled by the fall of one. Distress, bankruptcy, and liquidation follow, and after a few months, or years, the rubbish is cleared away, and a slow and tedious process of recuperation sets in. Economy again becomes the rule, and extravagance the exception. If the pendulum swung far and long in the direction of wild speculation, it will go with an equal momentum to the side of depression and stagnation.

Our most notable panics occurred in the years 1822, 1837, 1857, and 1873. Others, of much less intensity, somewhat different in character, in 1861, 1866, and 1869. That of 1837 was, perhaps, the most severe in its immediate results, and the most lasting in its after effects. It was ten years before values fully recovered and business resumed its normal activity. The principal antecedents were a great expansion of banking and bank credits, and an intense speculation in real estate, especially in New York City. In 1830 there were three hundred and twenty-nine banks in the country, with a capital of $110,000,000. In 1837 they had increased in number to seven hundred and eighty-eight, with a capital of $290,000,000. Prices of all commodities advanced rapidly, and industry and frugality were at a discount. Many abandoned agricultural pursuits and removed to towns or cities, to speculate in real estate and enjoy their rapidly increasing riches. At length the climax was reached, and the succeeding crisis occurred on May 10, 1837. Careful estimates subsequently made showed an actual shrinkage in value of the assets of the country of two billions, and an amount of indebtedness wiped out by actual bankruptcy, of six hundred millions. Complete specie resumption by the banks in all the States did not take place until 1843. Thousands, who thought themselves wealthy, lost all, and had to make a new beginning without a dollar. Labor was a drug, and all property unsalable, except at ruinously low prices. Values sunk as much too low as they had before been too high. Recovery was very slow and difficult. It required years of toilsome effort to ascend the same hill that had been descended at a single leap.

The panic of 1857 was, perhaps, next in severity, and the preceding conditions were very similar. The influx of gold from California, after its discovery in 1848, was added to the other speculative elements, and its effect was to intensify the passion for rapid gain. The severe object lesson of twenty years before had been forgotten, and history repeated itself. The prostration was not as severe, and the recovery more rapid than before; but yet the disaster was great, and thousands of fortunes were swept away. The suspension of specie payments by the New York banks, however, lasted only fifty-nine days. Recovery to the normal standard of business and prices was not quite complete in 1860, when the great political events occurred which led to the civil war of 1861. The opening of hostilities produced violent changes and irregularities in our banking system, which precipitated a crisis in the currency. This was quite unlike the panic of 1857, and much less severe. The bonds of various Southern States had been largely used in the North as a basis for bank circulation, and as their value rapidly declined, great confusion in our monetary system followed. Financial operations and exchanges were much disturbed, until the exigencies of the war forced the government to issue the greenback currency, which soon took the place of State bank issues. We are dealing with principles, and not history, and will only briefly notice these monetary changes and their effects. As the war progressed, the redundancy of paper currency increased, and soon caused it to sink below a gold basis. This movement grew still more pronounced when the national banking system was inaugurated, which was another outgrowth of the financial needs of the government. It was devised to aid in making a market for government bonds, which were made a basis for national bank circulation.

These issues, added to those of the government, caused a still further depression from a specie basis, until at one time their value was less than half that of gold. A corresponding inflation in all prices occurred, as rapidly as an adjustment could take place, and speculation was the natural accompaniment. As the volume of currency increased, its purchasing power diminished. Supply and demand must come to an equilibrium. There was, however, but little change in prices when measured by the gold standard, the apparent increase in values being in reality fictitious and artificial. Those who were sagacious enough to keep their assets largely in commodities during the expansion, profited, in case they turned them into money before the contraction. Thus, we meet the law of supply and demand at every turn, always uniform and supreme. The legislation of the Medes and Persians bears no comparison to this principle in unchangeableness. The quantity of circulating medium in any country has a direct relation to the price of its commodities.

The circumstances preceding the panic of 1873 were somewhat different from those before noticed. Its most prominent cause was an abnormal amount of railroad building. This is a laudable business, but it is quite possible to overdo it. There was also an unusual amount of real-estate speculation, and consequent inflation of prices. Whatever single feature may be the more direct cause of any panic, its effects spread to other enterprises, no matter how different their character. As a consequence, other values suffered nearly as much as those of railroad stocks.

By means of debt and inflation, current values of fixed forms of property became too great in proportion to the existing volume of real money. The disparity increases until panic comes, which merely consists of an excited bidding for money, by those who must dispose of surplus property. In their competition for money they offer an increasing quantity of commodities for it, which is called a fall in prices. A given sum in this way becomes more valuable, as measured by other property, in accordance with supply and demand. Wherever we turn in the business world, this ubiquitous principle is there before us. The potency of legislation is weak in comparison.

It is probable that the panics of the future, will be less severe than those of the past. Present business methods and conditions make it almost certain that no such convulsions as those of 1837 and 1857 will again occur. Rapid communication tends powerfully toward world-wide evenness of prices, and promotes the gradual discounting of what would otherwise be violent fluctuations. There is also a growing sentiment against excessive individual indebtedness, and business is more generally conducted on a cash basis. International commerce also conduces to steadiness of prices, and any abnormal prosperity or depression in one country, receives a corrective influence from other countries. There is a better understanding of Natural Law, and a more general appreciation of the certainty of the penalties for its violation. When all are familiar with unerring natural principles, and have confidence in their continuous operation, they will become less susceptible to impulses of fear and unreasoning panic. When a crisis is at hand, and exciting and disquieting rumors prevail, even the strongest sometimes lose their equanimity and reasoning power. Anything like a stampede in the financial world is most disastrous. Reassuring influences are very necessary at such times. Often a firm and united stand taken by the banks, with mutual assistance when necessary, accompanied by a temporary increase of discounts, will alleviate the worst features of a sudden financial crisis. A subsequent steady and slow contraction on the part of the banks, after the first excitement subsides, will generally take place, to conform to the changed business conditions. The greatly increased general foresight in determining the future tendency of market prices will do much to prevent any repetition of severe panics, for dangers foreseen can be largely avoided. Steady and even markets do not present good opportunities for speculation and rapid accumulations by the unscrupulous, but are favorable for labor, and all legitimate business and industry.

RAILROADS, AND RAILROAD CONSOLIDATION.

*"No pent-up Utica contracts your powers,
But the whole boundless continent is yours."*
Sewall.

"Facility of communication in social, commercial, and political intercourse is a distinguishing index of civilization."

*"Let observation, with extensive view,
Survey mankind from China to Peru."*
Samuel Johnson, 1709-1784.

XIV.

RAILROADS, AND RAILROAD CONSOLIDATION.

THE natural law of progress toward civilization and social development is by way of communication and transportation. These necessary advantages can only be secured by means of roads. A road is a symbol of civilization, and the lack of one, an evidence of barbarism. In countries without facilities for travelling from place to place, the people are poor and ignorant, and the government uncivilized and unstable. The road is the physical index of the character and cultivation of any age or people. It is, therefore, in accord with Natural Law, that the presence or absence of roads indicates a dividing line between two diverse conditions of society. When the Roman Empire was at the height of its power and grandeur, it was distinguished for its roads, and all led to Rome. Portions of the famous Appian Way, built three hundred years before Christ, remain to the present time. It was over three hundred miles in length, spacious, and smoothly paved with hewn stone blocks, laid in cement. Numerous other roads, equal in character to our best city streets, diverged from Rome for thousands of miles, to the most distant parts of the empire. Mountains of rock were tunnelled, and rivers and ravines were spanned by massive stone bridges, over which her invincible legions could march without interruption, while she was mistress of the world. These great works were so substantial that fragments of them still remain, notwithstanding the disintegrating influences of the frosts and floods of twenty centuries. In contrast, the feudal age of comparative barbarism was destitute of highways, and had no facilities for communication. The baron of old England, or on the Rhine, who ruled the adjacent region, perched his castle on inaccessible heights. He built no roads or bridges, for communication was not sought. Wheeled vehicles were unknown, except a few of the rudest sort, and all travelling was done on foot, or on horseback, through fields, forests, and streams. Then there could be no social or mental progress, no commerce, no activity. No industrial development or advance was possible, for lack of channels. By natural law, friction produces heat; so intercourse and intercommunication excite mental activity, and stimulate art, science, and invention. Nothing has so contributed to dispel the lethargy of ages, and to quicken the current of investigation, as the invention and utilization of the steam engine.

Even turnpikes were not constructed in England until the early part of the last century, and the first English canal was dug as late as 1760. The yearly movement of merchandise on al he through land routes of the world a century ago, would not equal that of one of our great trunk lines of the present time. Long-distance transportation by land, except for the most concentrated and valuable products, is entirely a thing of the present. We are more inclined to look at the present and future, but a brief retrospect is sometimes interesting and profitable. Not till 1833 was there a daily mail between London and Paris. The English postage on foreign letters was from twenty-eight to eighty-four cents, besides the foreign rates and ship charges to be paid by the receiver. On inland letters, at the same time, the postage was twenty cents per sheet. In our own country, up to 1845, inland rates were from six to twenty-five cents, according to distance. In 1851, a reduction was made to a uniform rate of three cents per half-ounce. Not only modern commerce, science, and literature depend upon easy and rapid communication, but even free government, except on a small scale, could not exist without it. Union of sentiment is indispensable to its continuance, and modern facilities of intercourse alone can secure it. The people of a vast territory, like our own, are more thoroughly assimilated and unified than was possible a century ago with those of a single State. The far-away provincial towns become almost like suburbs of the metropolis.

We soon become accustomed to modern facilities, and take them as a matter of course, and regard their usefulness with indifference. Not only so, but we often become exacting, impatient, and almost unreasonable in our demands upon them. The prairie farmer, who used his corn as fuel, for lack of transportation and a market, soon forgets his experience, and is dissatisfied with his present advantages. The railroad, which has doubled the value of his farm and products, and for the completion of which he ardently longed, soon becomes to him an offensive monopoly.

One hundred years ago, it cost three dollars to transport a barrel of flour one hundred miles; and salt, which was a cent a pound at a seaport, often cost six cents at an inland market.

A part of the price of all products is made up of their cost of carriage from the place where they were grown or manufactured. Often a slight decrease in transportation charges, creates new business, and enlarges that before established a hundred-fold, rendering necessary a large-increase in the labor required.

When railroads were in their infancy, it was assumed that they would be public highways, and that every shipper would use his own cars, or trains, paying the company a toll for the use of their track. As business increased, it was soon found that such a plan was utterly impracticable. The present clamor for restrictive legislation is perhaps a remnant of this antiquated idea, and much of that proposed is no more practical. A railroad is not merely an improved public highway, but is a great and complicated transporting machine, requiring the highest order of ability for its successful operation. We are mainly considering public interests, as related to railroads, but will briefly look at those of investors. We have seen that it is a natural law, that, as the interval between the investor and investment increases, the dangers from waste and mismanagement increase in like proportion. On this point, Mr. John B. Jervis, in his able work on railway property, says: "This kind of investment is not well suited in general to small proprietors so situated that they can exercise no control, and who are exposed to the danger of having their property managed by unfaithful men, who seek to make the institution subservient to their interest, rather than to that of the proprietors."

While restrictive legislation on the subject of railroad tariffs is unwise, and contrary to the natural law of supply and demand, there is a field for legislation which has received but little attention, and one as fully in accord with Natural Law, as legislation to prevent dishonesty, or breach of trust. We suggest enactments, making it illegal, with heavy penalties, for any railroad official, or manager, to buy or sell the stock of his road, except as an investment, and then only after public notice. He should also be required to make oath each year that he *has* not, and *will* not, make any speculative sales or purchases *indirectly*, or through any third parties. Here is a practical field for legislation that would promise good results. Railroad managers control a valuable *trust*, and if they profit by their superior knowledge, to the detriment of other stockholders, it is a moral wrong, which it seems proper to make a legal offence. The peculiar knowledge incidental to official position is, morally, as truly the property of the stockholders as the track or rolling stock. If fluctuations are produced by mutual combination, or understanding, among managers for self-profit, it partakes of the nature of a conspiracy. These great evils naturally cause that general distrust and suspicion which largely prevail in regard to official conscientiousness and integrity. Sworn statements, showing details of condition and business, after the nature of those made by national banks, should also be required at stated intervals. We earnestly recommend a trial of such legislation, which has a natural basis, instead of the artificial and impractical kind, which is opposed to Natural Law.

The remarkable movement towards consolidation, which has taken place during the last two or three decades, deserves attention. Popular sentiment is distrustful of such growing aggregations of capital and power, and some look upon them as an evil, and even as a menace to our institutions. The fact that consolidation is not only caused by Natural Law, but is also ruled by it, is entirely overlooked. If the process went on, until there was only one gigantic system in the whole country, it would still be subservient to the imperial edicts of supply and demand. If it made an effort to make artificial rates, or those that were even a little above the normal, then in a *greater proportion* demand would fall off, and business and profits would decrease. If a normal rate were restored, demand for service would be so much enhanced that financial gain would result. Supply and demand perform their office as quickly and surely as the "governor" of a steam engine.

The earliest railroad charters were for short independent lines. In England they averaged only fifteen miles in length. In 1847, five thousand miles were owned by several hundred different companies. In 1872, thirteen thousand miles were nearly all owned by twelve companies. This tendency has been nearly as marked in our own country. As a single instance, that part of the New York Central line between the Hudson River and Lake Erie, originally belonged to sixteen different companies. During the last decade the development has been, not merely into longer lines, but into great systems. Many of these now embrace from two thousand to six thousand miles of road, and form arteries through which commercial currents flow, giving life to great domains, each larger than some of the entire kingdoms of the Old World. What is the cause of this general and rapid consolidation; what its tendencies, and what will be its results? It has taken place not by chance, nor for any local or temporary reasons, but in obedience to the pressure and behests of unvarying Natural Law. The natural demand for decreasing rates for transportation, together with competition, have made it indispensable. It is a case of the " survival of the fittest," and of a development of the lower into the higher. In no other way could such remarkable reductions in rates and vast increase of business have been brought about. Under no other plan would such a degree of perfection in appliances and rapidity of service be possible. Modern convenience, comfort, and luxury are the result of the law of combination and consolidation. Contrast the present passenger service with that of thirty years ago. A passenger leaving New York for Chicago not only paid a much higher fare, but had to change at the end of each separate short line, and as often stand in line to get baggage rechecked and reloaded, subject to frequent lack of connection, long hours of waiting, and other numerous discomforts. One consolidated system, of a thousand miles in length, can render to the public a service which is immeasurably superior in luxury, cheapness, speed, and safety, to that which would be possible with any half-dozen distinct corporations.

Notwithstanding the talk of monopoly, rings, pools, and extortion, the fact remains that rates for both freight and passenger service are steadily tending downward, and will probably so continue. This is in obedience to the natural principles of supply and demand, and competition, and regardless of legislation. Greatly improved appliances, wielded by wider and more thoroughly organized control, cause the normal rates for service to decline, and natural principles are ceaselessly pressing actual rates into conformity. A normal rate is that point above which demand falls off so rapidly that profits diminish, and below which even a great increase of business would lessen them. The problem with railroad management is, therefore, to make the nearest possible approximation to it. It varies with every road, and with every different class of freight, and is a very complicated question, and one entirely beyond and out of the province of legal enactment. How much each particular variety of freight will bear, without in any way hindering its greatest possible increase and development, is a very delicate problem, and must be solved with great care. Legislation is futile, not only because price-making is outside of its province, but because no two roads are alike in business, location, cost of maintenance, character of traffic, and many other conditions. There is the same variety in these as in individual enterprises. To a very great extent, rates fix themselves, and the power of the management, in that respect, is greatly overrated. Suppose two or more competing lines enter into a "cast-iron" agreement to fix rates that are somewhat above the normal. How soon shipments "fall off," rival routes or water transportation compete, markets are disturbed, and speedily the "cast-iron" becomes sand! Take the extreme case of a road that has no possible competition. If even such a road attempts to impose artificial rates, business is hampered, settlement of tributary territory discouraged, manufactures excluded, and profits actually diminished. Railroad men have not yet all become aware of these facts, but they are rapidly learning them, and also that a broad and liberal policy is the most profitable. In no other kind of business is the old, familiar principle of "large sales and small profits" so applicable and profitable as in railroad transportation. The reason for this is that a large part of the expenses consist of "fixed charges," which are unchanged, whether the traffic be large or small. Outside of these, expenses increase much more slowly than the amount of business. An increase of twenty-five per cent. in general expenses might be sufficient for a business one hundred per cent. greater. A system of five thousand miles would probably not cost half as much to operate as it did formerly, when made up of a dozen distinct corporations. It has one board of management, instead of many; unity of purpose, in place of diversity; single and thorough organization, instead of inharmonious variety. The friction of one large wheel is much less than that of many small ones, and its power and momentum vastly greater. Consolidation should be considered as the greatest labor and expense saving process of the age. Why should "reformers" make such efforts to excite popular prejudice against consolidations? Is it simply because they are great? This is an age of great things, and of great privileges and benefits that are lightly appreciated. A demagogical cry of "monopoly" seems to be all that is necessary to arouse unthinking popular prejudice. The greatest possible consolidation is hedged in on every side by the impregnable, though invisible, barriers of Natural Law.

With constantly diminishing rates for service, and increasing safety, luxury, and rapidity, it has not yet been explained how the modern railroad can be a "menace," either to the citizen or to the government. Granted that sharp practice, stock watering, and many abuses exist, both in the construction and operation of these great thoroughfares. The systems are here, and to remain, and the public gets the advantage. Abuses are incidental to every enterprise, no matter how meritorious; and this will be the rule as long as the element of selfishness is dominant in human nature. Statistics show that, in a majority of cases, the first stockholders and builders sunk the money invested, and that the lines are afterwards operated by other and different proprietors, who purchased the assets at a nominal price. In general, no other investments pay as small a rate of interest as those in railroad property. Stock watering is indefensible as a system, but even here a candid view will show that, in some cases, it is only a "marking up" of nominal value to correspond with what has taken place in real value. The enhancement of market and taxable values, in terminal facilities and other kinds of property and improvements, is often considerable in a series of years. For instance: If the taxable and salable value of a road has increased fifty per cent. in ten years, is an increase in the same proportion of the stock by which it is represented in any way unwarranted or illegitimate? While this is the popular impression, there seems to be no valid reason why railroad property should be exceptional in this respect.

Another prevalent fallacy is that stock watering necessarily results in a higher tariff. We have already shown that rates are made by causes entirely different. If the nominal amount of the stock of any road was quadrupled, or reduced in the same ratio, its material property remains unchanged. Its earning capacities, surroundings, facilities, and opportunities are neither increased nor diminished. The normal rates at which business and profits are at the maximum remain as before.

Wherever there is dishonest and extravagant management, the investor suffers; but not the public, except indirectly. If unreasonable popular prejudice were gratified to the extent that, by unfriendly legislation, these great corporations could be crushed, it would be found that scores of small owners would be ruined as often as one "millionaire" was injured. A large majority of the stock and bonds of these corporations is widely scattered among thousands of small holders, including even many widows and orphans. The sagacious men, who, by their energy and capital, have given us these great facilities, had in view their individual profit; yet they deserve some honor, and not wholly reproach. Hundreds of millions have been lost by investors, the benefit of which is now being realized by the public. The commercial importance of these far-reaching systems is, perhaps, excelled by their moral and political benefit, in unifying all our diverse sections and interests.

The highest order of executive talent is required for their successful management. The chimerical plan that the control of these vast interests should be assumed by the general government, to be the sport of politicians, and to be fought over every four years, seems unworthy of serious consideration.

Cheap and rapid transportation has created new commercial centres, and millions of worthless acres have not only been transformed into productive farms, but have practically been moved a thousand miles nearer to market. The "long-haul" business is entirely a thing of recent times. The food products of the great trans-Mississippi region are found in the London market, competing with the productions of English meadows.

Art, science, and literature have all felt the quickening influence of this movement. Nothing since the invention of the printing press has so accelerated thought and investigation. With the aid of its twin sister, the telegraph, a nation becomes a vast neighborhood; and the pulsations of news, politics, morals, and religion are felt to the extremities. Mind attains increased preponderance over matter. These great modern appliances open the natural way of advancement, and hasten the evolution of higher general conditions from lower. By Natural Law, physical, mental, and moral attainment depends upon man's grasp and utilization of the forces with which nature's storehouse is overflowing.

THE CORPORATION.

"*While they are subject to abuses, they are great forces in production, and have their place in the economic functions of society.*"

"*Corporations cannot commit treason, nor be outlawed, nor excommunicate, for they have no souls.*"

Sir Edward Coke.

XV.

THE CORPORATION.

THE merits and demerits of business corporations are now the subject of so much popular discussion that it seems proper to briefly notice their relations to Natural Law. Civilized life and society are permeated by their operations, and we come in contact with them on every hand. Though they are fictitious personages, they have many real personal qualities. They build and operate our railroads, telegraphs, and factories, transport our persons and property, manufacture our goods, and give employment to our labor and capital. They are peculiar to civilized life and society, and are not found to any extent under other conditions. Their existence and importance are entirely due to the natural law of organization. In the physical realm, organization is a characteristic of life. It is everywhere present in nature, and forms unities which are composed of diverse elements. The human body is a unit, but it is made up of organs whose functions are dissimilar.

Those nations and peoples who possess the

genius for organization, and understand its power, are distinguished for the number and variety of their corporations. Such were the ancient Romans. No people ever more thoroughly comprehended the value of organization, and in Rome corporations had their beginning. The corporation of to-day, in England and America, is modelled after those which were so numerous and useful in the days of Roman civilization and dominion.

In general, corporations are divided into three classes: first, the municipal, or those embracing cities, towns, and villages, and having a variety of functions; second, the eleemosynary, or those which embrace colleges, schools, hospitals, and asylums; third, those of a commercial or business nature. As the latter belong to the department under consideration, we shall confine our attention to them.

Business corporations are creations of the State, formed for the prosecution of enterprises which cannot so efficiently be carried on by individuals. Their object is the public good, though formerly, in England, they sometimes conferred special and exclusive privileges. They have rights and obligations of their own, which are not the rights and obligations of the individual corporators. Their distinguishing characteristic is perpetual succession. A corporation can come to an end in three ways: by the death of all its members without successors, which is extremely improbable; by a voluntary surrender of its charter; or by a repeal of its charter by the State. Such a repeal is not held to be admissible in the United States, unless so provided in the charter, which is regarded as a contract between the State and the corporators. A corporation can make its own laws, provided they do not conflict with the general laws of the State. In some respects it is not as free as an individual. Its path is marked out, and it must follow it, while the individual is free to make any contract which is not unlawful. Its duties are defined by its creator, and it lacks the spontaneous, elastic, and impressible nature which may characterize the individual. Hence the adage that "corporations have no souls." On the other hand, it possesses great advantages over the individual in perpetuity, limited responsibility, and powers of accomplishment. His business closes at death, but this imaginary personage lives on. It is a name in which individuals act in specified ways and for definite purposes.

Few individuals could build a railroad or a great factory; but, if so, its business would have to be closed up or disposed of at death. Only by the natural power of organized effort can great enterprises be carried on.

The rapid increase, in number and variety, of these organizations, and their growing power, are suspiciously regarded by public sentiment. Here, as elsewhere, it is easy to confound abuses with the system, and to overlook great usefulness and adaptation to necessities. We vastly overrate their power for harm, even if they had harmful motives. Their prosperity, as well as that of their corporators, is bound up in that of the body politic. As producers they are entirely dependent on demand, and can oblige no one to purchase their products, unless he thinks it for his interest. As purchasers of labor or material, no one is obliged to sell to them, except of his own free will. Even if the managing power of a corporation had savage instincts, it is securely caged by the natural principles of supply, demand, and competition, which are stronger than iron bars. While the public is perfectly secure, stockholders are not always so safe. They are behind the bars, and sometimes need to be saved from their friends. For this reason, we earnestly recommend a trial of such legislation as is proposed in the chapter on railroads. It is suited to all kinds of corporations, and is in perfect harmony with Natural Law.

A corporation is like a colossal personality with magnified senses, or a powerful machine with every wheel and pinion adjusted to all its bearings. Each individual in the management is selected for his special fitness for the peculiar place, and he becomes an expert in the exercise of his function. Such organization has the strength and solidity of a pyramid. As regards their exercise of dangerous power, it should be remembered that they cannot sell their services or goods to an unwilling purchaser, and must court the demand they cannot coerce. Their transactions and contracts with others must be voluntary on both sides. It is, therefore, evident that a large part of the public distrust of them has its foundation in prejudice and demagogism, and also in the ignorance of natural laws which hedge them in. If corporations were blotted out, we should be set back a century in everything that pertains to an advanced civilization. Our great inventions and discoveries would fail of practical and general application. A better knowledge of Natural Law would dissipate many fallacies in regard to them, as it would also open our eyes to dangers that arise from its violation in other directions.

CONCLUSION.

" *All nature is but art unknown to thee ;*
All chance, direction which thou canst not see."
Pope.

" *Up, my comrades ! up and doing !*
Manhood's rugged play
Still renewing, bravely hewing
Through the world our way."
Whittier.

" *That very law which moulds a tear*
And bids it trickle from its source,
That law preserves the earth a sphere
And guides the planets in their course."
Samuel Rogers.

" *Facts are stubborn things.*"
Tobias Smollett, 1721-1771.

XVI.

CONCLUSION.

IS there a universal reign of law, and a fixed order of things? As far as the world of matter is concerned, all would probably give an affirmative answer. Fixed principles, relations, and results are well understood in physical science, and we are familiar with the properties of bodies, their causes, effects, laws, operations, and phenomena. That the realm of Natural Law is universal, including also the mental and moral nature of man and its operations, is not so generally understood. Nature and its laws must be taken as including all that is

> "In the round ocean, and the living air,
> And the blue sky, *and in the mind of man.*"

There is no spontaneity in nature. We must conclude that those events which are inexplicable to us occur in accordance with natural laws with which we are unfamiliar. It is but a step further to recognize such laws as the methods of the Creator. It follows that, wherever we can define and trace them, they are entitled to our respect. If they come from such a source, they cannot be violated with impunity. If we attempt to cross them, instead of walking in harmony with them, our path will not be a smooth one. If, therefore, the tendencies and principles which pervade the business world are subjects of Natural Law, they are worthy of our careful attention. If we have in any measure succeeded in interpreting them in the foregoing chapters, our labor has not been in vain. If the deductions made are in harmony with experience, with the known qualities of man's constitution, and are uniform in their effects and application, we are warranted in assuming that they are natural laws. For instance, we have found that the law of supply and demand is fundamental and universal, and that it is futile and injurious to oppose it. It appeared, that under all free conditions, these two elements will equal each other, and that the fulcrum upon which they are balanced is adjusted by price and competition, until the equilibrium is perfect. To oppose these natural forces has always caused trouble, and always will. They are like great ocean currents that move silently, but powerfully; and any attempt to obstruct them by artificial barriers will result in turmoil and confusion. Nature's methods cannot be equalled, much less improved upon. Herein lies the vital defect with labor combinations. Their conflict is not with employers or capitalists, but with the law of supply and demand. They are, apparently, not aware that their contest is with nature, and that it is impossible to overcome or repeal a Natural Law. Nothing but improved education will show them that those who goad them on in this combat are not their true friends. Demand for labor or productions cannot be coerced, but must be attracted and stimulated. The idea of a necessary and natural antagonism towards employers, is the foundation of all labor combinations. With that error for a starting-point, a whole system has been evolved. In the light of Natural Law we see that such combinations are unfavorable to individual merit and industry, and good production. Men learn to depend on the coercive power of the union, and not on individual merit. They become subjects of a tyranny, exercised by irresponsible tribunals, which order them "in" or "out," regardless of their own wishes and interests, and who lead them to persecute unorganized laborers whose legal rights and privileges as American citizens, are not inferior to their own. A strike which overflows its original limits, until it involves great public interests remote from the original cause, is a species of coercion whose damage is a thousand-fold greater than any possible benefit, even if successful.

Any impartial observer, who has noted the late writings and utterances of the leaders in labor agitation, will be forced to the conclusion, that these organizations are fast assuming the character of schools for the dissemination of socialistic ideas. It is a remarkable and significant coincidence that Congress, after trying many experiments for civilizing the Indians, has at last reached the true conclusion; that the one indispensable necessity is individual ownership of land; while at the same time our " reformers " are advocating a return to the Indian method of a general ownership of land. This must, indeed, be a singular kind of reform, which turns so sharply in the direction of barbarism.

We have found that labor is natural and honorable; that mental toil, not less than manual, is truly labor. We have seen that the theory, that the value of a product is based upon the exact amount of physical labor put into it, is fallacious; and that exchangeable, or market value, is true value. A lump of clay and a nugget of gold may have cost the same amount of physical exertion; but their value consists in what they can be exchanged for. It has also been shown that mental labor plays as important, and a higher part in production, than physical. Production is always the joint result of both. This disposes of the specious socialistic theory, that, as every product is produced by labor (meaning only physical), it should belong to the laborers.

The condition of the manual laborer, in this country, is not a fixed one; but his goal is the possession of accumulated labor, or capital. The road to this condition is open, and has been trod, step by step, by nearly all who have attained the desired result.

Man's nature is such that a tendency toward deterioration begins, and independence and self-reliance decay, when he depends upon anything outside of himself and his individual merits.

Employers have serious responsibilities devolving upon them. They should treat their employés like men, and not machines. A kindly interest in their physical and moral welfare is a positive duty, and tends to advance the interests of both, and of society. A system of profit sharing is worthy of trial, to harmonize interests that men have been taught to believe were antagonistic. Labor and capital can only prosper to their best and fullest extent, when the fallacy of antagonism is exploded.

It is plain that extra legislation is no cure for the ills of society. It cannot take the place of conformity to Natural Law. Official methods are cumbersome, wasteful, and subject to numerous abuses from the nature of the case, and should be limited to those enterprises which, from their public character, are properly beyond private control. The writer has no partiality for corporations; but he has endeavored to show that their power, and even their disposition, for harm, have been greatly overrated. Their interests are identical with those of the rest of society, and it should not be forgotten that they are the subjects of Natural Law, and in no respect its sovereigns.

We are aware that some of the conclusions arrived at are not in harmony with prevailing public sentiment, but we have made an earnest endeavor to sift out and retain the truth, regardless of its popularity. We believe that nothing is gained in the end by shutting our eyes to facts, even if they are distasteful to our wishes and opinions. Our work will, doubtless, be classed by some as one inimical to labor, because we have spoken plainly of the abuses that are done in its name. They are excrescences which disfigure its fair proportions. We are impelled to this work by a sincere regard for what we believe to be the best interest and prosperity of working men. We respect and honor them; but we do not indorse the schemes of their self-constituted champions. Many of them are, no doubt, honest; but we believe them mistaken. They have assumed, as a starting-point, the idea that there are two naturally and necessarily antagonistic interests existing in society. If this is true, their position is logical and correct. Our theory is, that society is a unit, like the human body, composed of different members, whose functions are unlike, but which altogether form a complete whole. *When one member suffers, all suffer; and when one rejoices, all rejoice.*

We have endeavored to prove that class prejudice, which is so persistently stimulated by labor leaders, is injurious to all, especially to the interests of the laboring man. We yield to none in sympathy for the poor, the suffering, and the dependent; and our only object has been to point out to them the road to prosperity and independence. Their condition can never be bettered by the envy and abuse of those who are more favorably situated, nor by blocking the wheels of business to coerce a demand for their services. We ask the thoughtful and intelligent laborers of America to be guided by reason, rather than prejudice. We warn them that many, under whose lead they are now marching, are giving them bad advice. If, in the course of these chapters, some unpleasant conclusions have been reached, we have been forced to them by the logic of unvarying Natural Law, and not by choice. We would like, most heartily, to see every laboring man in America have high wages, and steady work; but *nothing* can bring this desirable condition about, but industry, patience, providence, temperance, and public confidence. We have endeavored to do labor, as well as society at large, a service by these plain words. We invite all classes and interests to give them a fair and candid consideration.

www.ingramcontent.com/pod-product-compliance
Lightning Source LLC
Chambersburg PA
CBHW031825230426
43669CB00009B/1227